I CLOSED MY EYES

D0018224

I CLOSED
MY EYES

REVELATIONS OF A BATTERED WOMAN

Michele Weldon

HAZELDEN®

INFORMATION & EDUCATIONAL SERVICES

Hazelden
Center City, Minnesota 55012-0176

1-800-328-0094
1-651-213-4590 (Fax)
www.hazelden.org

©1999 by Michele Weldon
All rights reserved. Published 1999
Printed in the United States of America
No portion of this publication may be reproduced in any manner
without the written permission of the publisher

Library of Congress Cataloging-in-Publication Data

Weldon, Michele, 1958–
    I closed my eyes : revelations of a battered woman / Michele
Weldon.
        p.   cm.
    ISBN 1-56838-341-X
    1. Weldon, Michele, 1958–   . 2. Abused wives—United States
Biography. 3. Wife abuse—United States Case studies.   1. Title.
HV6626.2.W48   1999
362.82'92'092—dc21
    [B]   99-34356
                                                                          CIP

03 02 01 00 99   6 5 4 3 2

Cover design by Mary Brucken
Cover illustration by Stefano Vitale
Interior design by Nora Koch/Gravel Pit Publications
Typesetting by Nora Koch/Gravel Pit Publications

*For my mother, who urged me to write it all down, and
my father, who taught me to live life with an open heart.
And of course, for my magnificent boys,
Weldon, Brendan, and Colin,
who teach me that love can be pure and forever.*

Contents

Preface

"Will you ever forgive me?"

His voice was familiar, plaintive, beckoning in its mock sincerity. But now I was keen and unwilling to erase all that had come before. I knew this voice too well, the somber, innocent voice, the one that always comes after, the one that sometimes comes right before. I've heard it hundreds of times. And what he has done is not okay.

"No."

In a drumbeat, a denial. There was silence. And then he asked for a favor, to switch a visitation, to have our three boys longer than he is allowed by the courts. I said no. I will not forgive him simply because he demands it. I can possibly forgive him because I have grown to the point where it is better for me to release the pain. But not now, not that day. Not at his request.

His voice changed. He told me if I had sex I would be easier to deal with.

I have read shelves of books and magazine articles extolling the healing qualities of forgiveness, and I wonder. I know it is a popular notion. I know the nation wrestled with the forgiveness of a president. Television talk shows center on themes of forgiveness, bringing out guests begging for redemption for a scorecard of betrayals, hoping to be acknowledged as the audience pleads for a happy ending. I know that atrocities between people are forgiven as easily as coins of red and white striped candy are thrown from a float at a Memorial Day parade.

I know for many an apology embraced is freeing. But apologies are what imprisoned me. I cannot honestly absolve my former husband of the abuse. To say I do would be a lie. He dismisses all he has done as trivial, while the abuse, no longer physical, has transformed to verbal and emotional, playing itself out in bitter phone calls and seemingly endless litigation, with the children as pawns when convenient.

Forgiveness for me means absolution, wiping the slate clean. I cannot do that to a man who I feel deliberately and cyclically abused me. I do not hate him, but I am aware of who he is, and it is not excusable. What he has done to me, and continues to do, cannot be dismissed. Sometimes the only one you can forgive is yourself.

Forgiveness undeserved is what compelled me for one-third of my life, the twelve years spanning the time I was twenty-five years old until just after I turned thirty-seven. Nine years of marriage and three children all added up to a monument to forgiveness. And it was forgiveness that perpetuated the spiral, a forced compassion required to constantly understand and forever swallow explanations that were hollow and unworthy. I was moved further into this quagmire by my own driving desire to make my marriage work, to succeed at all costs, and to cover up the glaring evidence that this model man I married was not at all who he seemed. I see now that forgiving him is what granted the violence permission. Being the forgiving rubber wife is what allowed this to unfold.

Perhaps the word I need for him is not *forgiveness* but *understanding*. That may heal me. The anger does wash cleaner as time passes. It does get farther away, lost in the separateness of our lives, the wholeness I feel without him, the fullness of work that I love, and the business of loving my boys. The harsh, jagged edges of my rage at having been so duped and gullible are worn smooth by time and new experiences, but the rage is there, nonetheless. Ubiquitous, but tamed. The passion of my indignation has faded, bleached by the new, honest life I began the day he left.

I know it would be futile to say I will forget. I cannot forget that I was the victim of a hushed, private violence; it is as much a part of me as are my three small boys who shout desperately for my attention from rooms down the hall. To forget would mean to embrace the chance that it may happen again. My memories, aggressive and ravenous as tigers, will not let me forget. I can pray someday I will understand why he did what he did. I am beginning to understand why I accepted the violence, and it has not been simple.

Surviving domestic violence is like walking away from a raging fire that has consumed your home, your life, and your self-definition. You are plagued with the details of how this atrocious fire began, how it spread, and how it took so long for you to jump to safety. Sometimes it just starts with a forgotten match. And before you acknowledge the danger, your life is engulfed in flames.

In June 1997, on my thirty-ninth birthday, I came home from dinner with my friend Mariann, her treat for my birthday. I pulled my gray 1990 Volvo station wagon into my garage, pressed the automatic garage door button, and walked up the back stairs into the kitchen. I paid the baby-sitter for the evening and watched her through the window as she walked to her parents' car, parked at the front curb. I paused in the kitchen for a glass of ice with water, walked quietly upstairs, and kissed each sleeping boy as he lay in his bed.

Weldon, then eight, was in his room decorated with a sports theme, his favorite *Goosebumps* books lying on the floor where he had thrown them. Brendan, six, and Colin, three, were asleep in their beds in the room with the bright red farmhouse my sister had made for them. They looked small and peaceful, their blond hair brilliant as moonlight as the hall light shone on them.

I went to my room to put on my nightshirt and get ready for bed. Reliving the laughter Mariann and I had shared, I opened the medicine cabinet in my bathroom, reaching for contact lens solution. The glass and oak cabinet door, one in a triptych, came loose in my hand and fell on me, heavy and blunt, sudden, unprovoked; a thunder hit above the cheekbone and against my chest. My arms strained to keep it from crashing to the ground. I laid it slowly on the floor, against the gray-tiled wall.

Then, the past erupted of its own volition, memories I could not contain, like rubber snakes in a trick cannister.

The panic I knew from years of rehearsals raced through me, triggering that familiar fire drill. *Ice. Stop the swelling. Will anyone see? My face roared in pain, my chest throbbed. How will I camouflage it? Is there a cut? How big is the red mark, and is the white epicenter smaller than a dime, bigger than a golf ball?* I knew the routine well.

If I get the ice on it right now, this second, I can hold it down, I can fool the skin, I can pretend it never happened. Have I been able to deny a blow this big before? Concealer, blush, the thick matte foundation, maybe powder; the Chanel foundation won't work, it's too thin.

Desperately checking the red marks in the mirror, minutes fresh, I moved down the checklist, a path grooved from experience. Fingering the ice cube in a glass of water I had filled just moments before, I placed it cool-stinging on my face, grimacing at the stunning, frigid solution. *I can let the chest and arms go for now. I must hide what is on my face.*

And so I relived each hurt there that night, remembering who I fooled and where I was, congratulating myself on how clever I was to be such a master of disguise and deceit. *This isn't so bad. He isn't so bad. If no one sees what he has done, then no one will think he is a monster and I am a fool.*

The time in 1986 when he punched me on the chest in Dallas (he was just trying to stop me from walking away, and his hand accidentally was formed into a fist, he said), I wore high collars. The bruise on my arm from his bite after we had moved to South Bend, Indiana (when he was so angry at the progress of his own therapy he became infantile, the counselor declared), was simple enough to ignore in winter. In 1991, with two boys under two, I saw no one else during the day, filing stories for newspapers by my computer's modem. Play group with other mothers in the area was only once a week. I was away from my family. No one would see.

Also during our time in South Bend—during his first year of law school in 1990—we flew back to Dallas during his spring break. We attended the wedding of the sister of a close friend. We mingled, eating carefully fashioned hors d'oeuvres from silver platters served by young men wearing white gloves. We danced only hours after he gave me a black eye (the time, you know, when he just momentarily lapsed because we were staying with friends and our son was so young and law school was so stressful). I was quite sure our hosts had overheard, and Weldon, then one, was terrified, crying and clutching me. But no one had asked.

That night, I danced with the priest from Holy Trinity Catholic Church, Father Lou, who had counseled us in the Pre-Cana requirement before our own wedding. Even he did not know the pain filling my brown satin shoes. "Weldon hit me with the toy phone accidentally," I told him, I told them all. They all believed me. That my handsome, witty, charming, loving husband would act violently was absurd.

No one would believe me. I can't ruin our vacation. It will be fine. It will never happen again. Ever.

At his family's Christmas party in 1992, his oldest sister joked about my lip, swollen and blue-black from a blow he gave me December 24, after an argument about the Christmas rituals of our families. "Did he hit you?" She laughed at the insanity of the prospect and went into the kitchen to get me a glass of white wine, with ice. "No, Brendan threw a toy train, aiming for the toy chest, and I was in the way." This was my practiced response. "He is so strong," I said. "I bruise easily."

But just so you know, I wanted to say, *your brother did this because Christmas with our families is so tense.* "Can you pass the dip? Did you melt the cheese with the salsa or stir it in after? These egg rolls are so good." *Will you still love me if I tell you what your brother has done?*

And then there was the aftermath of the last time in 1995—though my husband did not know it was the last—when he came to me in our bed, the bed we had bought for our new home. It was four days after the last assault and two days before the morning in domestic violence court that changed our lives, the morning I stood up and spoke the truth about the man I married. Just before 6 A.M., he was dressed for work in one of the white shirts (medium-starch, boxed please) that I picked up at the cleaners dutifully every week.

He sat near me on the bed as I laid there, not having slept much or well, dreading another day with him in our house. He said impatiently, "Just write an apology for me. Anything you want me to say, and I will sign it." He refused to be the architect of his own contrition. I didn't do it, of course, but the wisdom of that choice often strikes me—in court mostly—that it would have been a great document for the file.

Only seconds had passed since the cabinet fell, but each memory was vivid and searing, demanding to be acknowledged as if it had happened just now, just then. And then I remembered where I was. It was my birthday, and he was gone. He had been gone for almost two years. Exhausted, I stopped reciting the excuses and reliving the fallout, the cover-up, and the victory of concealment.

There was no need to keep throwing the dice with a memory of another injury, long healed. This time it was innocent, an accident. The medicine cabinet fell. No one was to blame. He did not hit me this time. He was gone.

I cried loud and strong, the tears dropping fast and full on the floor, my voice making a sound of anguish so powerfully hoarse and deep it didn't feel as if it came from me. I thought that after he left our home and our daily lives, I would never be forced to walk through the checklist again, grabbing for ice, wondering who would see and whether they would know. I hadn't planned to ever feel this hurt again.

I sat on my bed, the same bed we bought together, but now in a new house and covered in all white: a new white duvet cover, all-white pillows, even a white canopy. I was claiming purity for myself, though I could no longer claim innocence.

So the boys wouldn't hear or be afraid, I closed my door and I kept crying. I cried for all the nights when I came into a room singing, only to leave hours later performing a triage dance of camouflage, spreading leaves and branches over a dark hole so no one would know it was there. I cried for all the women I met at the battered women's shelter, Sarah's Inn, where in our weekly group sessions, we shared the stories of men who seemed to be the same person. I cried that I had needed to take my children to a sanctuary for battered women, for help, for relief, to understand, to heal. I cried for the women on this Saturday night rushing for ice, hurrying themselves through their own checklists.

I was one of them, they were part of me: a sorority of good, kind, smart, trusting women who loved men who abused them. I cried that I knew a quick way to hide a black eye and that I had once thought love meant forgiveness was mandatory and unconditional, as it is with children.

My shoulders pulsed up and down as my insides released a howling, jailed horror. And then I knew that this hurt I was feeling would always be there, making itself known in the cabinets that fall innocently or the balls and toys the children throw that land here and there and hurt nonetheless.

I realized I was still wounded, like a soldier, and that loud noises or the sudden bruises recalled the gunshots and the grenades. They unleashed the wild dogs inside me who guarded my long-strangled secret. When I could breathe smooth and slow again and my chest didn't feel as if it would collapse from the weight of my memories, my tears stopped. I could be calm.

The honest answer to his plea for forgiveness, right now at least, must be no. But one day I may look inside and find the anger has burned away to ashes. I will live better, love honestly, learn well from the madness.

"I'm sorry, you know," he said brusquely once as he dropped off

Brendan after an afternoon visitation. He had been gone from the house a few months. He was ordered by the court to stay outside; he came in the house anyway.

I was not able to acquiesce on demand. "It's not okay. It's not enough. Are you sorry for hitting me? Are you sorry for ruining our lives? Exactly which part are you sorry for?" My hands were shaking.

"I'm sorry for it all," he said smugly, as if all he had done was spill a cup of coffee on a white carpet or track mud on the kitchen floor. He was smiling.

I didn't buy it then; I had grown immune to his apologies because they were followed, always, by new aggression, in whatever form it took. He would retreat in his attacks for weeks, sometimes months, then reappear, unprovoked, with new hostility, another fight, another battle, another twist of truth.

I may eventually forgive him. I am not there yet.

But I do forgive myself.

Forgiving myself for staying with a man who abused me has not been an easy act, an automatic assumption. It has taken every moment of the years since July 7, 1995, when the man I married left our home for the last time under an emergency order of protection. I have had to work hard to convince myself it was all right to stay as long as I did, that I did what I needed to do at the time. I had tried to make it better.

I was vulnerable, naive, blinded. I believed in a man I loved, and I did not believe he would keep hurting me. I stayed with him, and I chose not to see the man I married, the father of my three children, as a batterer who would always be a batterer. I saw each instance as an isolated nightmare, all explained away, all forgiven. I didn't connect them to see the pattern.

I excused his rage because I could not bear seeing him as he really was. That meant I would see myself as I was, and I refused to be a battered wife. But it was not until I could make that admission that the abuse could possibly end. It was not until I could say out loud what he had done that the carousel of pain would stop, and I could get off the painted horse and walk away.

Now I forgive myself for staying. I try to forgive myself for choosing for my sons a father who battered their mother, though that has been the most difficult. I forgive myself for trying so hard, for believing in something impossible, for having hope. I forgive myself for pretending to be happily married and pretending that a man who abused me just didn't know how to handle the demons inside him. I forgive myself all the excuses.

I can forgive myself because the game is over and he is gone. I saved myself, and I saved my sons. With only his occasional appearance, we are happy and whole, a family. I forgive myself because I can now fill my children's lives with new memories and laughter that I pray sustains them. These new memories include ones of a mother who is strong, a mother who loves them beyond measure, a mother who taught them that forgiveness is earned. I taught them, by what I have done, that sometimes you have to leave.

I taught them that it is never all right to hurt anyone; it is wrong to impose your strength on anyone else. I taught them and myself that it is foolish to think you can change another person's behavior, no matter how hard you try. I taught them to love with kindness, not control.

Forgiveness is a choice, always a choice. It is not a forced requirement.

Yes, I forgive myself, and writing this book has initiated the process. In speaking the unspeakable, in writing and witnessing the truth, the power of the secret is diminshed. I no longer carry the ghosts of domestic violence with me in every conversation, every act, every movement. I don't feel that I wear a scarlet letter *V* for violence.

I can be someone more than a once-battered wife. I have exorcised the terror of spousal abuse by writing it down. Jarring memories reclaim me at times of their own volition, and I know they are there. I respect them and the lessons they have taught me. I acknowledge their power. I am thankful sometimes for those memories because they keep me humble and remind me to be sensitive. On paper now, it seems so clear. It never did when I was living it.

My eyes are open. I will not close them again, look away, or deny what is right in front of me. I am conscious. I will not distill the truth and spin it so it no longer shames me. No longer crippled by my wish for a happily ever after or deluded by my self-deceit, I see what is there.

I have won because I have won myself back.

I claim me.

Acknowledgments

I could not write this book or even breathe freely without the help of my family. My mother has helped me in every way ponderable, as a guide, a safety net, a source of inspiration. My sisters, Mary Pat, Maureen, and Madeleine, are consistently centers for hope and laughter. They have done everything for me whenever I have needed it— from tutoring the boys in math to helping me when I am sick or even having us all for dinners. My brothers, Bill and Paul, are strong and soulful men, who not only care for me, but teach my boys through their example that fathers can be good and kind as well as gentle. My sisters-in-law, Bernadette and Madonna, have listened and understood, giving the shelter of their hearts and whatever else they could to help the boys and me. And though my father died before my children were born, I thank Papa Bill for the help he brings our lives daily. I feel his presence in every space of my life, and I know without hesitation we have his blessings.

My dear friends have done more for me than I could have ever hoped. Ellen Schofield was the closest to me literally and figuratively during the last few years of my marriage, helping me daily, even if it just meant giving the boys a bath after a long day. As my neighbor she saw my life unravel, a witness to all the pain and hurt, and a steadfast ally. Lorraine Iannello was with me—if only by phone regularly or in person once a year—helping me to reshape my life and regain myself, encouraging me to tell the story. Dana Halsted, my soul mate, helped me to heal, as I was coming out of hiding, as I began to tell the truth. Mariann Pushker was there to offer reason when I felt there was no reason left. Cynthia Hanson urged me to keep writing. Linda Berger was a source of spiritual calm, coaxing me to see beyond the hurt to what I could become. Pati O'Connor and Laurel Davis listened whenever I needed consolation. My colleagues at Northwestern University's Medill School of Journalism advised me during the arduous process of publication.

Perhaps the most important friend to the birth of this book has been Vicki Spina. She has offered her wisdom, guidance, friendship, and encouragement, believing in every dream I spoke out loud and helping me to name it.

Bob Vogt, my attorney through the hardest parts of this ordeal, has been a supportive friend as well as exceptionally competent and compassionate. At the lowest points, he persisted in his calm and helped the boys and me to prevail. I also thank Dr. Elisa Lapine for her guidance.

At the *Chicago Tribune,* Marla Krause gave me a space for my voice and hundreds of opportunities to tell my story out loud. A few of the chapters began as essays for the WOMANEWS section of the *Tribune.* It was good practice for writing this book and made me feel brave and accepted. I am grateful to Betty Christiansen, my editor at Hazelden Information and Educational Services, for so eloquently and heartfully encouraging me from the very start of this process. Writing about oneself honestly is a most difficult task.

To the staff at Sarah's Inn in Oak Park, where I went with my three children for six months to sort through the ordeal of leaving a violent relationship, I am exceptionally thankful. I am attempting to give back as a member of the strategic planning board for that wonderful organization. I felt some nights that just by driving to Sarah's Inn, my boys and I would be okay. My friends at Tuesday's Child, where I volunteer as a member of the board of directors, advised me on matters concerning the boys and offered me unconditional support in telling this story. Being part of that giving organization also helped me to sustain balance and perspective. The women of Children's Memorial Guild helped me to stay strong and other-focused, especially under the guidance of my sister-in-law Bernie.

To all the women and men I have met through my writing as well as speaking engagements, I thank you all for your soothing words of comfort. I thank you for your applause and your shared laughter. I understand your tears, and I thank you for trusting me with your secrets. To those of you who have shared your similar stories, I thank you for your honesty.

This book could only happen because of the people in my life who helped me to finally open my eyes, see the truth, and live honestly: my friends, too far-reaching to name them all, my family, and my children. Some friends' names I have changed to protect their privacy, though their support is ubiquitous.

This book is also for all the women I can never know. I pray they will read these words and know they are not alone. I pray they know they can not only survive, but live their dreams.

PART ONE

GETTING THERE

Card received on our fourth anniversary, August 23, 1990

Dear M,

My notion of love is swallowing the impulse to attack for the sake of what you might need. This love is not concerned about who is right as much as it concerns what you need and what I need. I think I went into this relationship with the embedded notion that love never has demands which leave me vulnerable. So when your needs left me so, I attacked. I had been helpless for so long I had no other response. That is changing. And that is what I believe is significant about our fourth year together.

In this past year I learned I will be a great success. I believe that as much as I believe you will be a great success. It's always seemed more obvious with you. But I've learned to love myself and that is your most precious gift to me. You have taught me my self-worth to a great degree. I will begin to repay you now with a steadily improving, increasingly uplifting marriage.

I love you. I love being married to you and I commit myself again to this beautiful life with you.

1

I Closed My Eyes

I closed my eyes.

Because I knew what was coming.

It was always the same: the air just before thick with rage, red-ripe with anger. I never watched when his hand flew toward me; I only waited for the sound of the strike—shoulders clenched, neck tight—as if all I was waiting for was a balloon popping or the brief, shrill cry when a child falls from a bike, outstretched hands scraping cement.

And when it came, I never knew where his hand went first, which way his fingers grasped me, which arm sent me to the floor. I could never answer the questions properly, the ones that I asked myself, only myself. I could only feel the throbbing and the stings, like battery-powered flashes across my face, sometimes my chest, an arm, a shoulder. And I mentally mapped the argument in bruises and splits of skin, the blood warm and wet, my cheeks puffing up to apologize like air bags upon collision, the truth suffocating within me.

In twelve years together, including nine years of marriage, there were repeated split-second eternities when the man who was my husband was someone I didn't know. And in those crimson flashes before each time he struck, I always remembered his eyes before I closed my own. Cold blue, pale as stone, the pupils wide, black chasms, his dark eyebrow arrows aimed at my face, his teeth gripped hard to his mission.

And before I closed my eyes, I held my breath, knowing that sanity does not hold court here. With my own eyes closed, the image of his eyes stayed before me in the darkness, like the square image of a television screen or the fading imprint of a lamp's white-hot bulb across the inside of your eyelids when you first surrender to sleep. In my darkness, I was swimming underwater, without sound and without weight, body-less, soul-less, lost, unable to breathe or speak or remember.

As soon as the sound came, I felt a relief in the distant place where he struck, for there was no more need to recoil, only recover. This was the end, not the beginning of it all. There was no more reason to be afraid. Today. Ever. *This has to be the last. This can't happen again.* The stinging radiating through my body reminded me that all I had to do now was heal. A different movie was playing, a slower soundtrack, with a woman's soothing voice.

I would cry without sound at first, the hole inside me so vacuous, so unforgivably hollow that the loudest knell could not penetrate its emptiness. I was already beyond it; I had flown past and above and could no longer be touched.

You didn't get me. My eyes were closed. It didn't count.

I closed my eyes, yes, I always closed my eyes. I didn't want to see him smiling. I didn't want to see what he promised he would never do again. And with my eyes safely closed, I could escape to the mountains inside me, the paradise he couldn't poison or devour with his words. I would find again the haven where I kept the kaleidoscope of colored drawings, where I could hear the songs inside me sing again, the tears heralding their own chorus of comfort. Inside me, I could feel the heaving breath of my children sleeping, soft as puppies.

I couldn't hear him, really; the sounds about him were muffled and strange, animal-like, sometimes cursing, sometimes whimpering, never quiet or calm. I could not attend to him for I was somewhere else, always, somewhere he could no longer touch me. The apologies would come later; they needed time to warm up.

The man with the cold blue eyes and the percolating apologies was not the same to anyone else in the world. He was a different man. Completely.

Handsome and convincing, he had once looked charming and regal in the navy blue Bigsby & Kruthers suit my mother had bought him to celebrate his graduation, cum laude, from law school in 1992. He was a litigating attorney in one of Chicago's largest firms, Sunday school teacher, mentor, all-around great guy, the kind of guy other fathers called to play handball, the kind of man who was just a little too intense in a Saturday game of basketball. He cheered at my oldest son's T-ball games and carried the children in the rain under umbrellas on Halloween, ringing all the doorbells. He called my mother on Mother's Day. He smiled in all the pictures and sent me flowers in colors so brilliant they eclipsed the bruises on my arms. He wrote me beautiful letters.

"Your husband is so wonderful," cooed more than one woman friend—envious and ignorant, part of the throng who knew us from church or work or the neighborhood—from across the social distance you keep when you want a secret hidden. "You are the perfect couple," I heard often. "You have it all."

He was even a good dancer.

Athletic, articulate, intelligent, funny—he seemed to be the perfect husband, the perfect father. I watched other women flirt with him, some innocently, and each time I thought, *If only you knew.* He delivered passionate soliloquies at parties about how proud he was of my career as a journalist, my accomplishments, my love for our boys, my ability to keep all the pins in the air. But behind the curtains, away from the crowd, I was juggling barefoot on shards of glass, spinning, tiptoeing past him, around him, to keep intact the wounds that would spill our family secret, hoping no one else would see.

If they find out, it's over.

"You talked too fast," he whispered in my ear once as I sat down at a starched white-linen table. I had just delivered a speech at the annual fund-raiser for Tuesday's Child, a nonprofit intervention program for children and their families, where I was on the board of directors. The hotel ballroom was moving with applause and cheers. I drank in the approval and absorbed the nods and smiles sponge-quick, eager to be liked, eager to be loved. He had to criticize.

They like me. You're wrong. Could I be married to one of the smiles instead?

"Psycho wife," he would sing to himself in the kitchen loud enough so I would hear. "Loser," he would call to me to underline a thought. And sometimes the taunts lasted until the moment the car, filled with our friends, honked in front of the house, beckoning us on a Saturday night. I wiped my tears as he walked brusquely past, pushing my hand aside as I tried to reconcile.

And then, only hours later—sometimes less—he could smile and lift a glass of blood red wine in a toast to tell all the world how much he loved me. And I prayed that this public face would become the face he wore at home.

Maybe if we stay out all night. Maybe, this time, he won't change back.

Because whoever this man was in private was someone I did not want in our house. Without him, his stress, his excuses, our house was filled with joy and promise for me, filled with the laughter of my women friends and our children. Our house was a mosaic of bold colors, flowers, and pillows I covered in silk and tied with ribbons, photographs of smiles, the picture of a happy family growing, the face of love, completeness.

In the kitchen the refrigerator was covered in crayoned pictures, and in the family room, toy boxes spilled bad guys and trucks. On the table in the breakfast room a bowl was filled with apples the color of love.

But with him it was often a completely different address, a scary place where my stomach tightened and my head pounded, hammering behind my eyes, hammering them shut. When the boys went to sleep, I did not feel safe.

He's dangerous. Get away from him.

I felt he brought the violence with him, his rage so palpable at times, it had its own seat at the dinner table. It took all my energy to avoid it and to pretend it could stay hidden. It was the monster under the bed, the bogeyman in the closet. His rage was the reason, in the last few months before he left, that I reached for the asthma inhaler when I heard his footsteps on the back stairs, the reason my hands shook at times when he called on the phone from work, the reason I rarely complained when he worked early and late, weekends and holidays. It was the reason I slept soundly only when he was away.

But I stayed. Married, committed for better or worse, and it was worse than anyone would ever suspect, worse than I would ever admit. Each day the violence, for years even just the memory of violence, eroded more and more of me.

I dreamed I didn't have a face, Mom. You gave me a small bag of bright fuchsia lipsticks, black and shiny in their containers, five in all. "Here, you love this color, dear." And I couldn't use them, Mom, because I didn't have a face. Where is my face? Did he hit it away?

I thought the proper response was to endure, to be a good Catholic wife, to help him through it, over it, under it, wherever the hell he needed to go to get away from it. I told myself I should stay to fix it for him, for the children, lastly for me. I would stay so I wouldn't be alone, so there could be a happy ending, so I could stop gripping the edge of the bed and praying he wouldn't touch me. Where were the sincere promises, the soul-baring letters, the words imploring me to love him, the eyes that asked forgiveness? How could it have come to this from such a happy beginning?

I prayed the terror would vanish as quickly as it came.

I chose him, at first, because he seemed safe. He was from a good Irish Catholic family. We were in the same high school class at Oak Park–River Forest High School. He graduated from a Catholic university, majoring in philosophy and literature, Great Books they called it. After a year in the seminary, he decided to be a writer instead. For God's sake, he almost became a priest.

He was a man with promise, a man filled with dreams I wanted to share. He was witty, captivating, smart, and strikingly handsome. He didn't smoke, drink, gamble, or do drugs; he wasn't even rude to strangers. He loved his sisters. He hugged his mother hello. He could admit his faults, and he was always so sorry.

When we started dating in October 1983, I was not looking to be saved, rescued, delivered. I was looking to love and be loved, have a partner, share a life, build a family. I had known him in high school and saw him again eight years after we graduated, on State Street. I was walking home from work, and he was walking to his late-shift job at a news service. I handed him a card with my home phone number.

Before our third date he said he loved me, on the phone from his office. I wanted the kind of deep, passionate love he professed. I was flattered he couldn't live without me. *Of course I deserve all this attention. Of course he fell in love with me right away.* He was infatuated, adoring. *I am this wonderful, so he must be too. Isn't everyone young and in love deserving of it all? Isn't it always this simple?*

For the three years before we were married, he was a man whose life seemed ruled by his love for me. I relished it and loved him back.

So I forgave the violence when it arrived, unannounced and without warning, three years after we started dating, shortly after we were married. I treated it as if it were only a minor transgression, like forgetting to take out the garbage or coming home long after dinner was put away in Tupperware bins. I forgave him because I didn't want it to be true. I only knew about violent men from television, movies, or an occasional talk show. The man I married couldn't be like them. That was impossible.

The first time he hit me was on New Year's Eve, 1986, four months after our wedding, when the world was silver-and-crystal perfect, and we danced to Lionel Ritchie songs and toasted to forever. I don't remember why we fought; perhaps the wine cost too much at dinner. I remember where we were—in the second bedroom of our duplex on Oram Street in Dallas. I remember he was wearing a brown suit, and I was wearing a black skirt, white silk top, black satin shoes; I remember looking at my shoes. I remember his eyes as he pushed me on the chest, his hand outstretched and hard, forcing me down as I lost my breath, lost my balance, and lost my trust. He had never hit me before. Afterward his eyes were full of tears. I wore turtlenecks to hide the bruises.

I'll do everything perfectly. I'll make my life full. He won't have to do anything. We can be happy.

Of course I accepted that I contributed to the argument, he made sure of that. Of course he was a good man who lost his temper. Of course we worked to break the pattern. I put all the flowers he sent in the living room. We took walks, we made love, we went to a marriage counselor. But it was never good for long, and it was never good enough.

He hit me again. And again.

It started sometimes as a slap, a sudden sharp-dagger movement, hitting my mouth, my eye, my nose, an arm. It could have been an argument over bills, a party, a misunderstanding, the boys. Sometimes he didn't hit me; he only raged. Once he mangled a blue wicker hamper because I cleaned the kitchen floor while he was reading the newspaper. The arguments always ended as quickly as they began. One strike. One hit. It was over. He would run away.

The counselors—three in three different states—each spoke in soft, generic tones, sometimes for $90 for fifty minutes and sometimes in rooms so small I wanted to vomit. There was Anne-Marie in Dallas in a pristine office in a stark boxy building with a tape recorder. In South Bend, there was Mickey, a university counselor, handsome and athletic, just like my husband. In Chicago, there was Father Gerry, the kind pastor who had known my husband's family his whole life. In each office, I stirred my coffee or bitter tea in a white foam cup and couldn't look at my husband playing the melody of deceit with his church voice. And each counselor said to contain the anger, be kind, be careful, tell each other you love one another. Be sorry. "Say the word *suitcase*," Mickey said, "when you feel as if you are about to blow. Have passwords."

After each time, we went to a counselor, and he sent more flowers, enough blooms to fill a cemetery. He let me sleep late on Saturday, made dinner a few times a year, changed the oil in the cars every few months. He brought me blouses from Ann Taylor and wrote me long letters. He put a patio in the backyard. He made new screens for all the windows in the house. He called our boys gifts from God. He recounted the moments when each child was conceived. He said he believed in me, and he said I was good.

I am not a battered wife.

But it began to occur to me, in the urgings from a small voice deep inside that I could not silence or avoid, that the good man with the bad temper was just a bad choice.

He has to know that what he is doing is wrong. He is logical, intelligent. It is stress. It is his own fury. It isn't me. He only hits me once in a while. I cannot only bear it, I can change it. I did not cause it, but I can solve it. I can make this man be who he says he is, be who I need him to be. I will make it all better. No one has to know.

So I would not tell. I knew that my close friends and my sisters would tell me to leave—no, make me leave. My friend Ellen knew the smallest part of the puzzle and wondered why I stayed, as she wondered why the whole family—even Colin—bristled when the garage door went up and Daddy was home. "Why are you still married to him?" my friend Dana asked.

I was afraid my brothers would hurt him back and my mother would pack our things and drive us away, with my boys screaming for their father. I was afraid of someone, anyone, seeing what really happened at our home.

What did you do to make him mad?

What would I say? Wasn't he the handsome lawyer? What was wrong with me? Wasn't I able to keep the family safe? I was ashamed to let anyone know what was happening to me.

I am not a battered wife.

I hated that I forgave him, that I was seduced by his explanations, his reasoning that his love was so vigorous it defied boundaries. "No one has ever loved you like this," he said, not knowing how true it was.

"I am a beautiful woman, and look what you have done to my face," I cried once.

"I am sorry your self-esteem is hurt," he shrugged, as if all he had done was drop a bottle of my makeup on the bathroom floor.

I hated that I forgave him—such a weak, chameleon move—like those weeping, pleading women in the country western songs, the lead roles in made-for-TV movies. Even months after each episode, when the apologies no longer hung between us like clouds, I could never answer the why. So I stopped asking it out loud. And in the weeks and months that swelled to fill the voids between the violence, what was real became blurred. It was just a blip on a time line once the bruises had bloomed past yellow and the blood had been bleached from my nightgowns.

I am not a battered wife.

"Pack your bags. Gather your children," I was told. "Violent men never change," the voice on the shelter hot line said. "Have an escape plan," the counselor in South Bend told me.

Get out. Your children are not safe. Do not stay.

But I did, and we went on to have three children, anniversary dinners, family picnics, and New Year's Day parties. And in these cramped parking spaces of hope and laughter, there was temporary shelter for my fears, the terror slipcovered neatly in promises. And he thought I forgot. But if I told my story to no one else, I told it to myself a thousand times.

With time, the unspeakable was no longer spoken of. I wondered sometimes if this handsome man—with our youngest, Colin, on the back of his bicycle in a baby seat, waving to the neighbors—was really the bogeyman I feared. I wondered sometimes if it all had ever really happened. If my eyes were closed, was I only sleeping? Did I remember it wrong?

"What happened in Dallas will never happen again," he told me as I folded the laundry in the basement just four days before the final blow. Which time in Dallas? The black eye? The bruised chest? The slap? I dared not ask. He seemed contrite.

But there were forever the black eyes and the fat lips to halt me, to distort the dream, to remind me this man was not at all safe. "A man hits you in the face," a police officer told me later, "because he knows you won't tell a soul." And I didn't.

Opening the presents on Christmas morning, 1992, the videotape shows my swollen lip. *Is this all you gave me for Christmas?*

There was the punch when I was five months pregnant with our first son in 1988. I locked myself in the small bathroom with the mint green towels, and I stripped off my clothes to take a bath. I saw myself swollen, my belly bursting with the child I craved. My image shook in the clouded mirror.

What am I supposed to do now?

I didn't leave then, compelled by loyalty and the belief that he did not mean it, propelled by the encouragement of Anne-Marie—who said we could stop the violence by being kind and by discussing the roots of the anger, as if any of it was my choice. I tried to believe, wrestling with rationality, suspending my fears that this man I loved was not married to rage.

I believed in him far beyond what was real, what was called for. I told myself he was not a violent man.

I can't be that stupid. I am not a battered wife.

I pictured the violence like a cloak, a shroud really, jet black, thick, consuming. I imagined it was something he could choose to wear (like the red tie instead of the blue one, or the brown shoes instead of the black) or choose to keep hidden in the closet forever. I pictured the violence as outside of him, as outside of us, instead of at his very core, welded to him, inseparable from him, a part that was immutable and not in my control. I should have known that a man who hits me once will always hit me. I should not have let my dreams overcome me. But when your life is covered in fog, you cannot see the exit signs.

And when your eyes are closed, you see nothing at all.

As the years wore on and hope became more forced, I kept loving him out of habit, out of loyalty, trying to keep the hurt at bay. I kept up the game, bringing the boys downtown to meet him for dinner, having his parents and family to the house for brunches, throwing parties for the law review staff where he was editor-in-chief, hearing his opening arguments in court, buying his secretaries Christmas presents. All the time, I kept my fingers crossed, hoping that he really was a man like my father, that he was gentle and that he loved me no matter what. I hoped that these instances of violence were aberrations, that he would change back for good, that each time was the last.

But there comes a time to stop pretending.

The soul, I have learned, has its own agenda and knows the truth even if you dare not acknowledge it. When the slaps, bites, and punches are long since anesthetized in afterthought, there comes a moment when, of its own volition, your soul says, "No more." You may not even hear it shout, or simply nod to its defiance, but it is there. And from that voice comes the solution and the strength, the voice no longer mute, the voice so clear it is deafening in its resolution.

There is a last time. And though it begins the same, the end is different.

At 10 P.M. on July 1, 1995, I walked behind my husband to the back bedroom of his parents' Wisconsin summer house to go to sleep. I had earlier placed Colin, who was one, in the crib in his parents' room. Brendan and Weldon were sleeping in the third bedroom facing the road. We argued. I told him I was angry he had made demeaning sexual comments about me to his brothers earlier that day. He wanted to leave to go to a local bar with his brothers and his old friends; I wanted him to stay to resolve the conflict. I wanted him to say he was sorry. In a half hour, we argued for what felt like forever.

"You hate me! Say you hate me!" he screamed, his teeth clenched. He leapt up from the bed where he was sitting as I stood above him, holding baby wipes in one hand and diapers in the other.

Lightning fast the air closed in between us. As always, I closed my eyes. Fingers cold and stiff as steel grabbed my jaw, and my mouth was struck before I landed headfirst against a wall. It happened in slow-motion darkness, like a B movie on pause in the VCR while the children slept; his mother watched a Dorothy Malone movie in the living room, and his father dozed on the front porch during the news.

The last time is different. After days and months and years of bandaging the violence, it suddenly failed to matter why. It was time to get away. It was as if someone else trapped inside of me long ago demanded to be set free.

I screamed.

In the black pool governed by my blindness, my eyes closed still, I was whole in the resolve that in spite of the confessions and promises no doubt to come, a resilience inside me was growing so cancer-fast that I knew it was over. And as I lay there on the cool white tile floor—blood filling my mouth, my jaw aching beyond movement, my head reeling—a part of me was joyful. *I will never do this again. I will never again be a battered wife.*

Footsteps came down the hall.

I will tell.

It was, after all, time to open my eyes.

Card received on June 6, 1993

Michele,

I love you immensely and I loved watching A River Runs Through It *with you. It was nice to connect last night.*

I wish you the very best for your dreams. I pray they come true. And they will.

2

The Perfect Husband

They don't carry signs, you know, even the worst of them, and there isn't an asterisk on their driver's licenses or the letter A tattooed on the soles of their feet. A man who becomes abusive does not have horns, drool venom, sweat poison, or even warn you that he is not what he seems.

No, he is most likely the one your girlfriends wish they had married. He is most likely the man in the room they all wish they knew better. He is most likely the charming guy who hugs all the ladies hello. I know my husband was.

When we first started dating in 1983, he was twenty-five years old making $8,000 a year as a reporter on the night shift of a downtown news service in Chicago. He lived in a two-bedroom apartment in Rogers Park with a friend named Carl who put holy cards on the fireplace mantle and kept peanuts in small glass bowls in the living room.

The man I fell in love with was attractive and charming, accommodating and sensitive, effusive and engaging, unassuming and honest. He was ambitious, having decided to become a writer after leaving the seminary and working as a bartender in San Francisco. I admired him for following his dreams and being willing to admit he had made mistakes and poor choices. He was refreshing.

Our first date was at a champagne bar. Other nights we ate dinner in my apartment on Cedar Street and took walks along Michigan Avenue, looking in the windows. We danced in the blues bars on Clark Street and ate Chinese food for lunch. We went to football games—the first was my alma mater, Northwestern University, versus the University of Illinois. We went to family parties: christenings, birthday dinners, weddings. Breakfasts at pancake houses, lunches in the park.

I dismissed the story he told me about the woman he had dated in San Francisco who was so crazy that once during an argument she hit him. *Boy, are you lucky you got out of that relationship.* I had never known a woman—or a man—who was violent, and I didn't know he was likely telling me that it was really he who had hit her.

Very open, he wanted to talk about anything, everything. In a quiz in the pages of a woman's magazine (the kind you only take if you are twenty-four or twenty-five and have the time for such things), he would have scored as "Mr. Right."

"He seems perfect," my friend Mariann said. "He can dance too?"

He would pick me up in his pale blue 1976 Delta 88 with the white vinyl roof, double parking and asking the doorman to watch it for him. His car was a gift from his parents, and it was wider than my first studio apartment. The car radio was usually tuned to an AM station that played jazz, swing, and forties music. There was something wholesome and endearing about him, his short brown hair, his wide smile, the way he made meatloaf for himself on Sunday night and five meatloaf sandwiches to last him through a week of lunches.

Clean and fresh like soap, he smelled young, innocent; he didn't wear cologne. His arms were strong and his build was thin, but muscular. He had sailed since he was a boy and later taught sailing at the Chicago Yacht Club. He was a track athlete in high school and a champion boxer in college. Once ABC-TV's *Wide World of Sports* did a special halftime report on him. He bore the physical confidence and lithe ease of a man who was exceptional in sports. The sailing trophies in his parents' basement were his.

He was a great kisser.

He seemed too good to be true. When my brother-in-law Mike met him for the first time in 1983, he asked with a smile, "Are you really as great as everyone says?"

He wore wing tips with khaki pants and button-down shirts. He didn't own a pair of jeans. He was a boy-man, dreaming and hopeful, not at all like the men I had dated before. He was not as sophisticated or polished, more vulnerable, inexperienced. He was younger than most men I had ever dated. I thought this was a good thing; he was less likely to be callous, dismissive. He seemed so young, so guileless.

A good dancer; God, he was a good dancer, and he would hold me around my waist, then twirl me. His movements were precise, controlled. I never danced with a man who held me so tight and guided me so closely. We looked good together. We looked in love. He quoted Homer's *Iliad* and nineteenth- and twentieth-century poetry from a college English class. He liked to watch the *National Geographic* specials on PBS, and I joked with him that he knew in detail how every species mated. He went to mass every Sunday and even said a prayer before eating when he came to my apartment for dinner. He went to confession regularly.

Only on occasion would he have a beer, a glass of red wine, or a screwdriver—just one, always, and he made fun of me at parties for drinking the kind of white wine that comes in gallon bottles with a twist-off cap. Having lived in San Francisco, he knew a thing or two about wine, he said. He could teach me.

I felt a brotherly comfort with him, but a definite physical attraction to him too. He looked more than a little like Kevin Costner, a young Mel Gibson, if you squinted to see. His face was smooth and welcoming, as if I had always been close to him, as if he was so comfortable he belonged with me, to me. His eyes were clear blue and serene at times, though he could be impulsive and spontaneous. He laughed hard and uncontrolled, loud, uncensored like a child. He was smart, really smart.

He made *me* laugh too. He was witty and thus filled all my requirements for a partner: smart, funny, handsome, and kind. My criteria never went any deeper than that because I had never thought it needed to. I never thought to include "nonviolent." I had never known a man who was dark or complicated, so I wouldn't have known what the warning signs were. I guess I skipped all those quizzes in *Glamour.*

We would meet some days for lunch on State Street at the Woolworth's that is no longer there; he liked tuna melts with milkshakes. My office was at State and Adams, seventh floor, the retail trade newspaper of Fairchild Publications where I was Midwest market editor. His office was on Wacker Drive, and his shift began at 5 P.M., so we would meet for lunch late before he began work. Sometimes we just walked, talking the whole time. I sat on his lap in the park near the Art Institute. We held hands. And kissed.

If there was a warning sign there, I couldn't see it. I guess I was too busy wanting him to be perfect, too busy nudging his quirks into the "positive" column. I wanted him to be like the men I knew were good: my father, my brothers, men with no surprises.

I did not know that men who tend to be abusive fall in love fast and want to spend all their time with you as a means of control. I just thought it was because I was irresistible.

One night after we had gone out for dinner, we were sitting on the beige Haitian cotton couch in my apartment. It was a tan-carpeted one-bedroom with a view of Lake Michigan possible only if you stood on a chair and strained in an unnatural position to see an inch of blue between buildings. On this night, he told me he fantasized about my apartment building burning down and how he would save me. I thought it very strange but sweet. I learned later it was about control.

We had been dating about ten months when I was offered a job as a feature writer for the *Dallas Times Herald.* It was everything I had dreamed of doing, but yes, I was in love with this man, and yes, I did see marrying him. He seemed perfect. *Should I leave without him? Would he wait for me?*

I didn't entertain the idea of not going to Dallas, of staying in

Chicago with him, so when he said he wanted to go with me, I was thrilled. Yet I was frightened by the burden of changing his life. I was afraid that if it didn't work out, he would hate me, his family would blame me. I didn't know that he would end up hating me anyway, no matter what I did.

He volunteered to move there to be with me, to quit his job, go to Dallas, get a job, and build a life with me. I remember a scene in his parents' Chevy station wagon, a ride back to Chicago from their summer home in Wisconsin, weeks before the move.

His father was driving, and his mother was in the front passenger's seat; we were dozing in the back. It was late; we had been to his cousin's wedding. The bride had worn a broad-brimmed white straw hat, and his youngest sister had told me she envied my new job, a life that seemed exciting. It had been a joyful night, another dreamy-eyed couple exchanging vows before the eruption of an enormous party outside on the lawn near the lake. On the drive home to Chicago, I closed my eyes, half asleep. The back window was open and the June air cool.

His mother asked him why he was moving to Dallas, and had he thought his decision all the way through? I kept still so I could hear what he would say.

"I love her, Ma, and I can't live without her," he said. "I need to be with Michele."

My heart swelled. It gave me chills. Those were romance-novel words, corny and exhilarating, ones I had waited a lifetime to hear. His mother had more practical questions about where he would live and work. He answered them dutifully.

Driving home that night in the safety of his parents' car, I was stunned by the belief that no one had ever loved me this much. *This is how it works,* I thought. *This is how my father feels about my mother. This is how his father feels about his mother. This is how it starts, and eventually you end up with a cadre of beautiful children and a house and jobs that you talk about over dinner, holding hands on the way to bed.*

And here is where it begins, the foreverness, the fruition of an ideal. This is the start of a parade of pictures on a mantle, the ones from the wedding and the ones from the twenty-fifth anniversary party. This is the script my friends and I rehearsed since I was four in our basement plays with Barbie in her white gown and Ken in his impossibly stiff tuxedo, his body without arms, his hair nubby. But this time, it was real. This was perfect.

I thought how lucky I was to be loved by a man this tender and giving, this kind and this determined. *He is as good a man as my father. We will live happily ever after.* The vision—paper thin and pasted to me—became stubbornly adhered at that moment, driving south on Highway 53. It was a vision I held tenaciously and would not relinquish, even years after it was clear that this man was not who he seemed. I held on to that vision even when it was evaporating and the untruth of it threatened to erase me.

But that warm, glorious night, with the windows open and the car rumbling fast and the calming voice of his mother distant and soft, melodious, dreamy, his arm on mine—there I felt loved. *This must be it. Nothing has ever felt this good.*

I was twenty-six in the early summer of 1984, and some of my friends already had gotten married. From where I stood as a brides-maid in all those satin dresses—eleven in all—it looked so easy. You marry the one you are dating in your twenties. Just as in a board game, you land on the marriage square when you have moved enough spaces, counted off enough turns. Everyone wins. *It's about time,* I thought, as if I was on a schedule. *I'm on the right square.*

I felt part of the club, the esteemed sorority of women who had husbands, fiancés, or boyfriends who could only see them as trea-sures, who never saw the flaws, who never complained about din-ner or having to take out the garbage. Who never made a cutting remark.

The partners for life. The perfect husbands.

Card received on our eighth anniversary, August 23, 1994

M,

Can you believe it has been eight years since I raised my hand in joy walking out of Saint Vincent's church? Eight years and three beautiful sons. We have been so blessed.

I love you.

3

Fiesta Forever

Moving to Dallas in July might not have been the best idea. It was blow-dryer hot every morning and suffocating at night. The evening we stepped off the plane and into a life together, it was 103 degrees. I learned not to touch the steering wheel of the car after it had been in the sun for more than an hour, and I set the thermostat in my apartment on Gaston Avenue to 64 degrees. The city seemed strange in its sounds and its smells, its small town-ness and its hulking, empty glass buildings. People talked differently in sharp, slow Southern accents. The pickup trucks had gun racks. There were drive-through beer barns and jokes about Yankees.

But I had work that was nearly perfect, writing stories that filled me, and experiences that were new, meeting almost every new experience with a man who loved me. The people I met at the newspaper were like characters from a play. I had a column called "Michele Weldon's Glitter Gulch Gossip," so I was invited to parties, concerts, openings, balls. I wrote feature stories and profiled celebrities I flew around the country to interview. I wrote about authors, actors, advocates, anyone in the eighties with an idea to push or a product to sell. From a distance, my life was charmed. I even spent a week in a suite at the Savoy Hotel in London filing stories about the marriage of Margaret Thatcher's son, Mark, to Diane Burgdorf, the daughter of a Dallas businessman. I was happy.

What could go wrong? For the most part, there had been an ironed, protected smoothness to my life and the lives of the people I knew. With few exceptions, I was not struggling; the pieces came

27

into place as expected. For someone who moved through the world predictably, with a gelatin ease, there is a danger of being insulated and oblivious, of being blind.

It will all be perfect, I thought. *I will have this perfect job and this perfect boyfriend and this perfect life. He will become a perfect husband. I will be the perfect wife.*

My boyfriend rushed to fill the still, dark, vacuous holes left by the absence of my family and my close friends. Like water pounding into an empty cavern, he flooded the spaces of my life and did not leave me air to breathe. I thought it was love.

He wanted to be near me every second. I craved his company, his closeness, his attention. We would talk a dozen times a day, have lunch together, meet for dinner. Delirious and young, we would kiss and plan and dream, planting the passion for a lifetime that would be as good as we dreamed. He read my stories in the paper and came to all the black-tie dinners in a tuxedo he bought secondhand just so he could be with me. Sometimes he was called Mr. Weldon at events. He said it didn't make him that mad.

He got a job immediately in Arlington, Texas, at a small daily newspaper on a recommendation from one of my professors at Northwestern University. It was a thirty-minute commute to Dallas, and he lived in an apartment on Pioneer Parkway with a loft and a stubborn population of roaches. But it was an adventure, our adventure.

I missed my girlfriends and my family. I missed my parents, my sisters, and all the birthday parties for my growing school of nieces and nephews. He was thrilled to be away from his family, and from mine. "Now we can work on our relationship alone without the pressures of your family," he said.

"Your parents hang on every word you say," he told me once after a dinner with my mother and father at the Drake Hotel's International Room before we moved. "It's disgusting. Your mother finishes your sentences, and your father sits there as if everything you say bears the wisdom of Buddha." He said he was repulsed.

"They get a kick out of me," I said.

It turned into a circular argument about the kind of person I would become if everything I said was treated with such blind reverence. I ended up apologizing and saying that I knew he was only trying to make me a better person. I dismissed the notion that he was a jealous ass.

Over the months and years, he met my friends, and they mostly liked him and thought he was suitable enough, if a little intense. When Dana, my roommate and closest friend from college, visited from Los Angeles, he was nervous, awkward. He later told me it was because he wanted to kiss her, that she was beautiful and exciting. He told me he loved me so much he could be completely honest with me. "All men really think this way," he said. I was furious, but I guessed I never knew a man as sincere.

Lorraine, who became my closest friend in Dallas, worked at the newspaper with me and lived two doors down in an apartment complex on Gaston Avenue. She and I spent hours talking about him by the apartment pool and debating if he was the right one. What did we know? We both decided he was worth the minor trouble: his possessiveness, the jealousy he denied but was there nonetheless, the intense arguments out of nowhere about nothing that lasted hours. I mean, he was cute.

Lorraine and I compared him to my brothers, her brothers, our male friends, old boyfriends. He came out ahead on some of the criteria and fell short on others. Still, he was a nice boy from a nice family. What could go wrong?

Lorraine and I both thought it was strange, though, that he called her and a handful of my other women friends when I didn't come right home after work one night. I'd gone to the Galleria in North Dallas to do spur-of-the-moment shopping, which Lorraine knew (I'd told her on my way out of the office) and explained when he called her, frantic. I was gone two hours, tops.

By the time I got home, he had left a half-dozen messages on my answering machine. Lorraine first thought it was weird, then said, no, he's really protective, he's just concerned about you. I never went anywhere again without telling him exactly where I was. I didn't want him calling everyone in the phone book every time I went to Saks Fifth Avenue for a sale.

I told myself I had nothing to hide, that he was welcome in every inch of my life. *He wants to be part of my life, all of my life. I must really be wonderful. Nobody has loved me this much.* We started talking about marriage.

One year after we met, the first Christmas that we lived in Dallas, he asked me to marry him. He gave me a white gold and diamond ring with a large stone in the center, diamond baguettes and sapphires on the side. It was his grandmother's, a keepsake of his mother's mother, and his mother had helped him to get a larger diamond—one carat—placed in the center. I loved it; it was part of his family, and through it, I felt part of his family. I had known his sisters and brothers my whole life. My mother had given bridal showers for his sisters, and to his parents I had offered cold shrimp with toothpicks at dozens of parties in my parents' living room. His father was funny and his mother was beautiful. I wanted to be loved by them.

His proposal was planned and ritualistic, not a surprise. After both of us flew from Dallas home to Chicago together for the holidays, we arrived at my parents' house in River Forest and retreated to the basement. I sat on the yellow chintz couch, and before me he knelt down and said he would love me forever. He asked me to marry him, pulling the ring from a blue velvet box in his gray tweed coat jacket. I put it on my finger, and then he called my parents downstairs to tell them the news I had told them months before. They'd just been waiting for the signal.

My father hugged him and then me, calling me "Mich," the way he had when I was little. My dad walked over to the bar at one end of the wood-paneled basement and from the wine cellar pulled out a small, dusty bottle of red wine, dated 1958.

"Here, Mich, I bought this for you when you were born. I have been saving it for tonight." I was astounded that this gentle, gracious man had moved this bottle from house to house, placing it high on a shelf and remembering the gift he would one day give me, his fourth daughter, his sixth child. He loved me enough to hold a secret for me and to share it when it would be the most special.

We toasted each other with raised glasses, and I took pictures, my father with his arm around my new fiancé, both of them smiling as wide as monkeys. Here are the two men I love most in the world, I thought. How could I be so lucky?

My mother hosted an engagement party a few days later, with an accordionist, my husband's family, my family, great food, and champagne. We took a lot of pictures and set the date for October, the Saturday before Columbus Day. My mother and I talked about Waterford patterns and bridesmaids' dresses.

We catapulted on, young and determined, making plans, working hard. Months passed. He seemed edgier, more tense, but blamed it on another new job, this time as a reporter for a small weekly business newspaper in Dallas as a reporter. On April 4, six months before the wedding, he told me he could not get married now. To say I was not devastated would be a lie. He said he still loved me and wanted to marry me eventually, but I told him I would only wait six months, and I gave him back his ring.

"Don't let me hate you," I pleaded with him when he pulled away after dropping me off at my apartment that night.

I see it now as the first in a litany of betrayals, yanks of control. He later said he felt out of control of the wedding and wanted it to be more about what he wanted, about us and less about ritual. I guess he resented the Waterford pattern my mother picked. I guess he disapproved of the invitation's script. I couldn't sleep well for days and stayed awake wondering how I got here, how he could have made such a rash decision alone when it was about me, about us. I was so confused. The dream was fading.

My sisters Mary Pat and Maureen came to Dallas the first weekend after he canceled the wedding, an ambassador's visit to cheer me up. We went to dinners and I tried to be brave. I tried not to cry, but my heart was shattered. There were days I forgot to eat. I worked long hours and went home and watched TV. I made a lot of long-distance calls. His sisters wrote me kind letters.

As the weeks and months passed, I became less angry and more trusting. I tried to go on a date with another writer I had met and spoken with at parties, but I made it just for lunch. Still I felt dishonest, as if I owed my boyfriend my loyalty. *He moved here for me. We've been together for nearly two years. He loves me; he only asked me to wait.* I didn't want to lose him.

I will do what he wants.

It was the first time I forgave him for hurting me, and it was certainly not the last. I never understood his reasons; nothing dramatic had happened. We continued to date, though mostly on Saturday afternoons; anything else seemed false. Yet he still called me his fiancée whenever I was introduced to his friends or someone from work. I was confused. My editor at the newspaper called it classic cold feet.

In early September, a few days shy of my six-month deadline, he asked me if I would wear his grandmother's ring again. I said I would only if we set a date and if he would not change his mind. I would not forgive him a second time, I said.

I did not want to be engaged forever. I had known women who had been engaged for five, six, seven years, only to have their fiancés go on vacation, meet a woman skiing or on a beach, and marry her a month later. I was not going to be a fool. We set a date; he was convinced now it was the right thing, and we targeted our lives toward August 23, 1986. He seemed sincere. I told my parents. My father said he would have to talk to him in person before he agreed. I was still on schedule, though, still on the marriage square.

It will be all right. He will be the perfect husband now. There will be a happy ending.

We went together to Marshall Field's in the Galleria to pick out the china: Villeroy & Boch, a cream pattern with peach marble trim called Sienna. He had opinions on the crystal, Mikasa, and the silver, 20th Century from Reed & Barton. We toiled over the booklet for the wedding, Psalm 88, "With my chosen one, I have made a covenant," was his choice for the front cover. An artist friend of his drew two doves beneath a cross, an image borrowed from one of my favorite passages from William Shakespeare's *King Lear:* "We will sing like two birds in the cage." Then I saw it as a symbol of love and commitment.

Three of his friends who were priests—an old friend from his childhood, his roommate from college, and a friend from the seminary—all stood on the altar and helped to concelebrate the mass. People joked that there were almost as many priests as groomsmen.

I later wrote an essay about our wedding for *Bride's* magazine: "We had a church wedding followed by a formal, seated dinner for 230 people. Like the many inner circles of a tree's bark, friends and relatives formed rings around the dance floor. There were cousins, aunts, and the girls I have been friends with since the age of eight. My parents' close friends were there, as were friends of his family. I had never felt as happy or loved—not only by my groom, but also by my parents, his parents, and all the smiling faces in that room wishing us well."

Our wedding photograph was published in *Town & Country* magazine alongside a collection of other black-and-white photographs of attractive, jubilant couples. While he smiled, handsome and bright, his pose always struck me as odd. He had a tight grip across my left hand, covering all my fingers as well as his grandmother's wedding ring. It is a forceful hold, and in the photograph I look oblivious. I wonder now if any of those other couples there in those pages with us, captured in a yesterday of bliss, have felt this kind of pain. I hope not. I pray not.

I gave him a gold wedding band with the inscription "Fiesta Forever" after our favorite Lionel Ritchie song, "All Night Long," the one we heard on our first date. He lost his wedding ring a year or so later at the health club, and I replaced it with another gold band with another inscription. He lost that too. I didn't bother to have an inscription on the third.

But that Saturday afternoon in August 1986 was perfect. We walked down from the altar, freshly wed, where he had cried at our vows, tears falling to the tops of his cheeks. Then he raised his hand in a fist and held it there, the defiant, jubilant conqueror, as the string quartet in the balcony of Saint Vincent Ferrer's Church in River Forest, Illinois, played "On Eagle's Wings." I tugged at his arm, embarrassed, but let him go. He was impulsive, after all.

I didn't know that he was telling the world that he now had control over me. He had won. It was a sign, like the thousands of other signs I chose not to see. It was a sign that for the next nine years he would continue his pose as the conqueror, as the victor, and I as his victim.

It was the signal that I was now married to a man who would tell me he wanted vacuum marks on the rug when he got home from work. Who would tell me driving home from the doctor's office in 1988, where I found out I was pregnant with our first son, that with this news he was sure my mother would now control our lives. This man would later tell me that my job was to take care of the house and the children and that everything else in my life, including my work and my writing, was mere distraction.

Here was a man who would hit me on Christmas Eve. Here was a man who would hit me when I was pregnant with our first son. This man would tell me he didn't want my friends from high school in our house. And here was the sign that the man I thought was perfect would wound me more physically and emotionally than anyone I would ever know.

"Please, God, let me kill her," he said nearly ten years later, six months before I obtained the emergency order of protection that led to the end of our marriage.

But that August afternoon, with my friends waving and smiling and the photographer taking pictures, I entered into a life I could not have prepared for. This man's presence would later make my stomach tighten and my heart pound just by hearing his key turn in the lock. This man would loathe me.

Here was a sign. But I only saw the handsome man in the gray-striped cutaway morning suit telling the world he loved me and that he was triumphant. He won me. I was the prize.

Card received on Christmas Day, 1989

My dear Michele,

I am so proud and thankful to be your husband. Not only do you inspire with your commitment to career goals, but your love of Little Man and the generous spirit you show others is beyond reproach.

Our Marriage continues to evolve, though I often disappoint myself with regressive anger or an inability to sort out my feelings. Yet in the aftermath of those resultant fights, I see my love for you. At no time, even in the loudest or most stressful confrontations does this realization of my love for you waver. My hopes for this year are a healthy Little Man, a blessed new baby and growth for you and I together and individually. For you, I pray your dreams come true in a flourishing career as a writer and success with the outpouring of your ideas. God has blessed you with an unparalleled creativity that often awes me. I also pray that you learn to care for yourself with some of the zeal that you care for others. Perhaps frequent massages, naps, workouts and other important health habits could become part of your 1990.

4

What Did You Do to Make Him Mad?

The phone calls began on a Thursday in July 1986 to my desk phone in the features department at the *Dallas Times Herald*. My phone rang a lot; calls from appreciative readers and subjects of stories, some calls from angry readers upset about a point of view, some from people who were desperate to have their names, companies, or causes in the newspaper. Sometimes it was friends.

When these new phone calls began, the caller identified himself as Michael Walton, a name the Dallas police later say he used because it was similar to mine. He spoke in a prolonged Southern drawl, slow and deliberate, telling me how much he liked me, how much he loved me.

It was your classic crank call.

Just like every woman I know, I had been answering obscene anonymous calls since I was a teenager. I got them in college, and I got them in every apartment I ever lived in, in spite of unlisted phone numbers. Sometimes I think there is an army of men out there who just dial numbers all day and night, hoping a woman answers.

He started calling a few times a week, not saying much, just how much he liked me and wanted to meet me. "I just have to be with you," he slurred. I wasn't all that worried because I wasn't in the phone book. He couldn't find out where I lived.

Call me all day long at work, buddy. You can't get me.

Then the same voice started calling me at home. He left messages, long and rambling, on my answering machine. I saved them.

This went on for weeks in the hot Dallas summer, but I was getting married August 23 and had many other things on my mind. *Maybe it's not the same guy calling me at the office. Maybe it's a different weirdo.* He had a different name. Now he was Mark. But he sounded the same.

One evening he called when my fiancé was at my apartment. I handed him the phone. The caller told him he loved me and just wanted to talk to me. The caller repeated, "I just have to be with her."

My fiancé said, "No, man, just leave her alone." He said he was spooked; he said the caller sounded nuts.

Great.

I was beginning to feel unnerved, queasy.

The caller mentioned in one message left at my home that he wanted to come to the office to see me. So I brought the tape from my answering machine to the newspaper and spoke with my editors and the head of security to make sure no one I didn't know could come past the front desk or be told where I was. They assured me no one would be allowed in to see me. There was a front desk on the first floor with a security guard and a receptionist in the hall outside the features department on the third floor. Even if he got past them, he would have no idea where I sat in the newsroom with close to fifty people at desks splayed across the room.

I felt safer.

Then, after listening to the tape, the head of security told me that it sounded as if the caller made the phone call from the loading dock at the back of the newspaper building. My building. They recognized the sounds of the presses and the trucks. They surmised that this stranger might have gotten an employee phone book from hanging around the newspaper. That would explain how he got my phone number at home.

He had been in the building. Now he knew where I lived.

I was scared. I didn't know what this man looked like, whether he was black or white or brown, young or old, large or small; his gnarled Southern accent was difficult to understand. I didn't know whether he was watching me. I would not walk across the street to the parking lot alone after work. I did not work late, as I usually did, and I did not go in on Saturdays when pretty much anybody could get in. I tried not to be swallowed by panic. I tried to reassure myself that it was just a weirdo caller and that nothing else would happen. Still, I was wary.

It was just weeks before our August wedding, and I was already nervous about that. But my fiancé reassured me he would protect me from anyone. He was an ideal knight. I didn't tell my mother; I was afraid she would be upset or make me come home where she could protect me. Years later, I was just as afraid to tell my mother my husband hit me. I didn't want her to be upset, even though I knew she would protect me.

But this was before our wedding, before I had ever felt the rage of a puzzling anger, of a violence aimed at me. I did not understand what danger was, but I felt the oddness of it, strong and thick and nauseating, a wind stirring inside, making me breathe faster, look over my shoulder, and walk as fast as I could anytime I was outside. Just as in the movies.

Danger does not belong in your life; it is an intruder, uninvited and unwanted. Danger is about strange little men who call your phone number by accident. Danger, I believed, goes away when you lock your door, pull the shades, and tell the security guard to protect you. Danger and violence can be prevented if you are cautious and you are smart. Violence comes from outside your real life.

The calls continued for weeks until one Thursday when I left my apartment on Gaston Avenue for work after 9 A.M. Apparently, the man who called himself Michael came to my apartment later that morning and waited outside my front door for several hours. The landlady, Carmella, asked him who he was, and he said he was my boyfriend. She said she didn't think so. Then she called the police.

The police came and questioned him, but he insisted to them he was my boyfriend. The landlady called me at the office to tell me the story. Ringing someone's doorbell is not a crime, the police told her, and maybe he was my boyfriend and I just wouldn't say so. They let him go.

He had done nothing wrong, the police told me later over the phone. His name was Bruce Jacobs. I could not prove it then, but I knew this was the same man who was calling me. It had to be; nothing else made sense.

I felt like I couldn't breathe.

I remember the terror of being a young girl in Chicago when Richard Speck killed those eight nurses in their apartment. I remember practicing with my sisters how to hide under the bed if Richard Speck ever came into our home. I remember reading newspaper stories of Son of Sam, John Wayne Gacy, and Ted Bundy, and I remember the horror I felt thinking of how your life could end because of a stranger, a stranger who doesn't look crazy, someone you trust briefly.

Violence and danger came from strangers, not people you know, and certainly not people you love. If you protect yourself from strangers, they can't get you. You are safe. No one who knows you, and certainly no one who loves you, will ever hurt you.

The next day Bruce Jacobs came back and broke into the apartment of my next-door neighbor. She was an older woman with impossibly dyed red hair who chain-smoked cigarettes, stayed in her apartment with the thick lime-green curtains drawn, and spoke with a tar-choked voice like gravel in a food processor set on low.

She said she came into her kitchen Friday morning and found a small man crouched on the floor with a kitchen knife in his hand. When he saw it was her, he ran out the back door. My neighbor later identified him as the same man who had been hanging outside my door all day, the man the police had questioned. It was Bruce Jacobs.

The Dallas police later said he must have thought it was my apartment he was breaking into; he chose hers by counting windows from the back of the complex and calculating the corresponding apartments. My neighbor had an extra window. With our kitchens flush to each other, the window he sneaked into should have been mine. But it was not.

I did not sleep there that night; I slept at my fiancé's apartment on McKinney Avenue. He came with me to pack some things, and as I was throwing clothes into a tan overnight bag hurriedly, I cried so hard it was difficult to see. I remember clearly thinking that if I had been home when Bruce Jacobs had come, I could be dead right now. I was only there because of the extra window. I was only alive because this stranger, this unknown madman, went into the wrong kitchen. He counted correctly, but there was an extra window to stop him. The extra window saved my life.

The line between life and death was so clear to me; it was there in my apartment, just inside the casement windows, almost visible, tangible, like a rope to keep you in line at the movies. If I had gone to work late, if I had stayed home, if he had counted differently, I could be dead. The insanity and randomness of it horrified me. The bareness of that realization clung to me like a suffocating noose. It was a feeling I had never experienced before. Though I was quaking in my confusion, the clarity of that one thought was numbing. Someone was trying to hurt me. I could have been dead.

A few days later, on July 22, Bruce Jacobs went to the University Park home of another woman whose name and picture he had seen in the newspaper. Though she was not a writer, she'd had a story written about her for ethnic dancing in the "Dear Dallas" column.

From what the police and special prosecutor told me, Bruce Jacobs climbed in the bedroom window of this woman's home, saw her in bed with her husband—both of them asleep—and became enraged. He then went into the father's sixteen-year-old son's bedroom and stabbed him dozens of times—I think the count was close to fifty. As the boy struggled and screamed, his body banged against the door so his father couldn't reach him. Jacobs ran out the door and into the night, leaving the son dead and these loving, innocent people to wonder why.

The murder story was on the local television news the next morning. A cab driver who picked up a strange little man near the address of the murder called the police to say he had a fare who was very suspicious, and the timing would be about right. The police went with the cab driver to the place in Oak Cliff where earlier that morning, he had dropped off a very odd little man wearing a dark cap.

From what the prosecutor said, the cab driver pointed to the spot where he dropped off the man, and there he was, wearing the same clothes the driver had picked him up in. What the driver had not seen in the dark was that the clothes were covered in blood. It was Bruce Charles Jacobs, a thirty-nine-year-old dishwasher at a chain restaurant in Dallas where he had harassed a waitress. The police arrested him, the same man they had let go from my apartment, the man my neighbor had seen.

After the murder, I never stayed at my apartment on Gaston again. My fiancé and I found a duplex on Oram Street, where we would live in the first floor of a house. It was a brick house painted gray with a fenced-in backyard and a magnolia tree. The landlady, Marcy, was kind. There were blue shutters and window boxes on the outside that I later filled with pansies in the fall and marigolds in the spring. The floors were oak, and it was air conditioned. There was a separate dining room, two bedrooms, and a den/alcove we later used as a nursery.

This was to be a safe place, where harm couldn't get to me, to us, to our dream. This was to be a sanctuary where danger did not exist and nightmares were held at bay. You need to be afraid of strange little men, not anyone you know. I would never have to be afraid of someone again. Lightning does not strike twice. I was safe now and forever, amen.

My fiancé helped me move all my things in extreme haste. We put clothes in large black garbage bags as my friends Lorraine and Andrea packed my kitchen. I wanted to move away from the violence. I thought I was.

Protection, I thought, *I will be married to my protection.*

In a swift trial in June 1987, Bruce Jacobs was found guilty of murder, and I was scheduled to testify at his sentencing. The prosecutor was seeking the death penalty, which he received. In Texas, the land of the good old boys and the Bible's eye-for-an-eye philosophy, if you kill someone, well, then, they kill you right back. The distraught father, who had been celebrating his son's sixteenth birthday that terrible night, testified about meeting face-to-face with Bruce Jacobs in his home that night. "I thought about trying to attack, and then I saw his eyes, and they looked like Satan," the *Times Herald* reported. "I had the feeling I was looking at Satan through the eyes."

The police said that Bruce Jacobs had my newspaper articles taped to the walls of his apartment, as well as the article about the woman whose stepson he would later kill. I had never seen this man before in my life. Nor had she. Sitting in the courtroom as he was brought in, I was stunned by his stature. He was a small, pasty little man, his skin butter-yellow and sallow, his movements sharp and quick, rodent-like.

My new husband was with me and kept his arm around my shoulder, even covering my face with a notebook so Bruce Jacobs would not look at me. He was there to protect me, to keep me safe.

How can you know whom to be afraid of? Bruce Jacobs was a complete stranger, an elfin man. If I saw him on the street, I would never look twice; I would not check my purse, cross a street, or pick up my pace. This was a man who did not look dangerous, a man who seemed harmless. But he was a man who killed a stranger—violently and without provocation—and he could have killed me. *He wanted to kill me.* I never imagined I would hear those words nearly a decade and a lifetime later from my own husband.

But that day in the courtroom, I cried in the arms of my husband. I cried for the parents, their murdered child, and for me. My husband told me he would always protect me. He said he would never let anyone harm me.

I forced myself into adopting a definition of safety that was black and white, one where harm came from strangers, odd little men who read your columns and taped your pictures to their bedroom walls. I told myself that safe is about family, safe is how I always felt growing up. I hid with my sisters under our beds to hide from Richard Speck—after he was caught—and I never worried about anyone I knew or loved hurting me.

But I also learned that violence has its own timetable and its own boiling point. I did nothing to provoke Bruce Jacobs but live and work with my name in a newspaper. Violence can erupt without any input or cause, a combustion from an internal flame. It would later help me understand the man I married.

"What did you do to make him mad?" my mother-in-law asked me July 1, 1995, the night in their summer house when my husband hit me and I screamed out loud.

What had I done to make Bruce Jacobs mad?

What does any woman ever do to be abused?

I have tried to understand this pervasive, eternal question, and I wonder if it isn't simply because logic requires us to think life happens in terms of cause and effect. It is too terrifying to believe that violence can be unprovoked, that men like Bruce Jacobs hide in their apartments with your address in their pockets without you even knowing who they are. It is too frightening to think perfect husbands become abusers of their own accord.

The victims of violence, especially women, are routinely blamed. It is an infuriating reality, but a reality nonetheless. I do not blame his mother for her question, it is a question that is embedded into the culture of centuries of generations. To think that violence would happen without two-sided responsibility is too threatening a concept. To think your own son, your own husband, is solely responsible is too much to even contemplate. Things that shouldn't happen don't, not unless you ask for them.

I didn't ask for Bruce Jacobs to stalk me. I didn't ask for my husband to hit me. No one ever does.

In 1986, the year I was married and the year I was stalked by a murderer, my vision of the world was simplistic. I could not understand why this violence had screamed into my life, why this threat had devoured my sense of safety. But I feel now that it was a baptism, an initiation. It was a lesson forcing me to define what is safe and requiring that I relinquish my sense of control.

I had no control over Bruce Jacobs. Years later I would acknowledge that I had no control over my husband. The violence was his, he owned it, and I could not contain it. I could not run faster than it, I could not work around it, no matter how many beautiful children we had or how many great dinner parties I threw.

Violence, I learned, is illogical and unforgiving. Like a fire, it spreads where there is air and space and where it is allowed. It is consuming and it is deadly, and it will defy boundaries even if you aren't the one who lit the match. Violence in the home is an encompassing, ruthless intruder. It will burn you and your children, and it has little to do with provocation. It rages past you and through you no matter how you try to pacify it, no matter how much water you throw in its path. It can never be enough. It feeds on itself. And it can kill you.

What did you do to make him mad? What had one woman done to make Bruce Jacobs mad enough to kill a son? What had I done to make him want to kill me? What did I ever do to make my husband want to kill me?

What did you do to make him mad?

The question incenses me still.

Card received on January 2, 1988

My dear Michele,

I am so sorry about your father's illness. I know how much he means to you, how your love for him is rooted in your daily happiness. The void and the pain you feel wears on your face. Let me continue to share that pain with you. This is our first suffering of family tragedy together. It is so devastating not only because of your feelings for your father, but because even our intensity, our love is challenged. This pain is opening up even more intimate channels in your heart and it's frightening for both of us. But we believe in each other's goodness, and will always be there for each other.

The gifts I bought you, a pretty blouse and a stretchable skirt, might prove perfect for our next dream—a child. Let's not lose sight of how we will express our love through a family. And let's not forget our love for each other is the most precious thing we have.

Love.

5

Ice-Cream Sodas on the Hood

The underbelly of an armadillo. That's how I described my father. He was a successful businessman with a tough exterior, but to his family, and especially to me, he was tender, vulnerable, gentle, kind, without armor, without defense.

When I was about five or six and we lived in the house on the 500 block of Clinton Place in River Forest, I didn't know what my father did at his office, just that he went there every morning at 7:30 and was home at 4:30 every afternoon. I knew there was a factory part to what he did and that his secretary was named Lillian, but I didn't know what they made in the factory. My mother said once that my dad made money. For years I thought he worked in a mint.

We had dinner every night about 5:30—the eight of us sitting around the breakfast room table on wrought iron chairs with yellow seats—and the only offering my father ever objected to was chicken. He hated it. In the army, I guess, where he was enlisted from 1942 to 1944, he had to pluck chickens, and it turned him off poultry forever. I think chicken was the only thing my dad ever disliked.

I sometimes wonder if it was World War II that shaped my father to gentleness. It terrorized his generation of men, teaching them that at any moment they could lose their lives, lose it all. Why create your own problems? My father's close friends all seemed so calm, so wise. They were children of the Depression too, knowing since they were young that in one day, everything could change.

Maybe they didn't dare behave in a way that would electively shake the havens they knew. They wanted their worlds to be simple respite because the external world could be so unpredictable and final. So many of their friends had died in the war. Why make your own war at home?

My dad was easygoing, smart, and funny, and he loved my mother generously. At Christmas parties he would sing, "O, Tannenbaum," a tribute to the part of him that was German. My parents kissed in the mornings before he went to work and again at night, and he called my mother "Patsy," a name no one else called her. You could see the love in their eyes.

We all had rituals associated with my father, none of the daily routines—my mother took care of those—but the special ones, the exclamation points, the territories that were Dad's alone.

We lived a few blocks from the Prince Castle/Cock Robin hamburger and ice-cream parlor on Harlem Avenue, and every few weeks we would have ice-cream sodas as a treat for all eight of us. Dad would go pick them up and bring them home.

It usually was my dad who ordained it an ice cream night because he had an insatiable sweet tooth. He loved hot fudge sundaes, banana splits, and angel food cake with homemade chocolate frosting. If you were lucky enough to be chosen his accomplice on soda night, you walked around the house rounding up orders and writing them down. "We're getting sodas," you'd shout upstairs, to the basement, to my sisters' room in the attic. And everyone would emerge, no matter what they were doing before.

My mom usually ordered peppermint ice cream, Dad and Mary Pat got chocolate, Maureen and Bill got butter pecan, Paul got banana, sometimes peppermint. Madeleine usually said no to dessert, but she could be pressed into sherbet. Wanting to be just like Madeleine, who was four years older than me and beautiful, thin, popular, and brilliant, I opted for a sherbet cone too, and it came with three layers of flavors—lime, orange, and strawberry. You would write down the orders: six sodas, two cones.

The carry-out sodas came in tall paper cups, like the ones for soft drinks, but with whipped cream and a cherry and long spoons. Tops wouldn't fit, so they were covered with a tent of plastic wrap and a rubber band. Getting them back home was a feat. If Dad chose you to accompany him—and most of us begged to go with him—you were part of the game, the challenge to get six ice-cream sodas home without a spill. The ice-cream cones you carried upright and gingerly in the car, holding your breath.

The teenagers behind the counter knew us well, and they would put four sodas in one cardboard carry pack, two sodas in another, then hand us the cones. I usually picked up a lot of extra napkins. I would glance down at the black-and-white tile floor, scuffed from the day's traffic, and I'd be careful not to trip or miss a step.

Driving the few blocks from Cock Robin (there's a McDonald's there now), Dad would put the cardboard carry containers on the front hood of the car. This innovative idea occurred to him after they all spilled inside the car once, and Dad decided it was easier to throw them out if they fell off the car than to clean ice cream, chocolate sauce, and whipped cream off the white interior of the mulberry Lincoln Continental or the white Chrysler wagon. This was the game: Dad would place the containers in the center of the hood of the car and drive home slowly—about five miles per hour—through the alleys to our house. His foot was just off the brake; he barely touched the gas.

If I was his aide, I would be charged with watching the sodas and making sure they did not tip or slide. He would drive so slowly, so carefully, saying the whole time, "You got to be careful. You can't go fast. You can't have a bump."

It was so much fun just to be with him and hear his voice, play his game, so absurd, so ridiculous. But being his secret ally in the silliness, sharing his intense concentration to avoid a mishap, being his partner in delivering the family's treats, that was the joy.

"We made it," he would say when we pulled into the driveway. He would carefully put the car in the garage, take the sodas off the hood, and bring them inside. As best as I can remember, I never saw him spill one with this method. He was too cautious.

When I was in fifth grade at Willard School in River Forest in 1968, I entered an annual Father of the Year essay contest, a Chicago tradition in all the schools across the city. I was a finalist that year, one of the top ten. I remember writing that my dad loved vegetable soup and that he was kind and always had time for me, even though I was the youngest of six. I didn't write about the ice-cream sodas because I thought it would be too hard to explain. Besides, how my father got the ice-cream sodas home was a deep secret at our house.

There was a dinner at the Palmer House downtown for all the finalists and their families, and I sat at the table with my family, my dad, of course, and my teacher, Miss Daus. We ate prime rib and baked potatoes with huge balls of fresh butter. There were prizes of tickets to a Chicago Cubs game, as well as coupons and a plaque my father hung on the wall of his office. The mayor, Richard J. Daley, was there.

I was the youngest finalist that year, and I really thought we'd win because I knew I had the best father. They announced the winner at the podium; it was a seventeen-year-old girl whose father was in a wheelchair. A lot of crying, hugging, and clapping ensued, but I was angry. I was sure it would be me; it would be my dad.

My father leaned down to me and said, "Mich, the guy is in a wheelchair. He'd have to be a great father. He deserves to win." He was matter-of-fact, not at all disappointed, but I was jealous. He applauded loudly.

"I don't have to win," he said. "We're here and that's pretty good," he said. He put his arm around my shoulder and kissed me on the top of my head, to the side of the bright green bow that matched my bright green patent leather purse and shoes.

My mother is the person in my life who took care of all the details, but my father was a separate kind of inspiration. My mother drove us everywhere. She organized my schedule, helped us all with homework, got us ready for school, made our meals, and talked to the teachers. She was the woman I wanted to be when I grew up.

I would see her transform on a Saturday night and take on the romantic smells of mysterious adult evening adventures, the Chanel No. 5 perfume that she dabbed neatly behind her ears and on the insides of her wrists, and I would learn how I wanted to be. She wore powder and silky slips and a red ribbon suit, the kind Jackie Kennedy wore in *Life* magazine. She was witty and competent and wrote my father's speeches for conventions when he was president of the Automotive Parts Rebuilders Association (APRA).

It was my father who made Saturday afternoons great, who would cut the lawn while my brothers swept the sidewalks, who would have talks with me or wait for me as I rode my bike around the block. It was my father who had intriguing destinations like the Ace Hardware store on Chicago Avenue or the Sears, Roebuck & Co. on Harlem and North, where we bought shiny and mysterious tools or supplies that clattered in the bag. He was strong and gentle, patient and persistent. Some Saturdays we would go out to buy lunch for the whole family, getting a dozen cheeseburgers at the McDonald's drive-through window and eating at least an order of french fries in the car before we got home.

I loved talking to him, hugging him, even listening to him talk to my mom in their secret language about business and taxes and meetings and friends. He had wise answers for homework, even if some of them turned out wrong in school the next day. "Ocean breezes" was a common response for anything having to do with weather or geography. He had stories to tell, stories about him, stories about being in the army in Europe, stories about being young and happy. Stories about us. Stories about my mom.

When I was a teenager and we had a summer house at Stop 22 on Lake Michigan in Long Beach, Indiana, my Dad and I would walk for miles up and down the beach talking. I would talk to him about school or boyfriends or my dreams. I told my Dad I wanted to be a writer, and he never flinched, criticized, or told me how hard it was. He told me I could do anything. "Mich," he'd say, and just the sound of his voice signaled a flow of relief through me, "you'll do great."

My father helped to center me; he was calm and uncomplicated, never too emotional, but always steady. A hug from him could last me a month. But it would never be that long before he would give me another.

When I was in graduate school at the Medill School of Journalism at Northwestern University, I spent the summer quarter of 1979 in Washington, D.C., working on a news service. I had a temporary desk in the Department of Agriculture's press room, the same one assigned to a Medill student each quarter, and on my desk was a phone. I called my father in Chicago every day at the company's 800 number.

I would check in with him at his office in the morning and tell him what I was writing about that day. I would tell him where I had been, what I knew, and how I felt. He would talk about my mom and what my brothers and sisters were doing. Then I would talk to my mom who had started helping my father in his manufacturing company while she worked on her MBA. She wanted to know if I was eating right, feeling well, and happy.

I loved calling him there because I could visualize him precisely, in his office, with the pictures of all of us on his desk and on the wall, and the paintings I had once made for him, the paintings Madeleine and Mary Pat made too. You couldn't walk into his office and not feel that this was a man who loved his family. This was a good father. This was a kind husband.

I called my father at his office less frequently in later years, from my desk at the *Dallas Times Herald.* When I moved to Dallas, my father asked often, "How long are you going to stay down there?" He asked it coolly, but I knew it was because he wanted all his children near him, not just on holidays. Not just for phone calls.

"Soon, Dad," I would say.

It was not soon enough. My father had a stroke on December 14, 1987, when he was out to dinner with my mother and some of their friends. He suddenly could not speak when she asked him if he liked his dinner. He was unable to cut his meat. She took him immediately to the hospital, and he never came home. None of us was prepared, my mother the least of all.

He was in a coma at Northwestern Memorial Hospital the last few weeks and had suffered a series of stuttering strokes as they called them. He could no longer swallow or move. They had moved him out of the Chicago Rehabilitation Institute because he would never improve, the doctors said. I had decorated his room there with small silver ribbons for the holidays. There were pictures of us on nearly every surface and get-well cards from the grandchildren.

My father died on January 18, 1988, four days after his sixty-fifth birthday. I was back in Dallas after returning from seeing him in the hospital on his birthday. My mother called with the news about midnight. I knew when the phone rang—before I even answered it—what had happened. It can only be bad news when the phone rings at midnight if you're waiting for your father to die.

At the funeral mass at Saint Vincent Ferrer, the same church where we were married, I stepped to the rose marble podium and read petitions I had written. My father's close friend, Duke, eulogized him. My father-in-law was a pallbearer. My husband was there, mostly silent, and my nieces were crying. My mother wore a navy blue dress and long jacket and said she couldn't feel her legs moving when she walked. At the wake, my sister Madeleine and I had kept our backs to the coffin. We were okay as long as we didn't have to see him there, dead. Someone remarked how good he looked, and was wrong. I had made the mistake of reaching down to touch his face there in the coffin, and years later I can still feel the roughness, the immobility, the coldness, the granite death.

For months after his death, I would dream about having conversations with my dad, and he would be kind and helpful, just talking to me as if we were chatting about anything, everything, a normal day. When I woke in the morning after a dream, I would feel as if I had been with him. During the days I felt his loss in everything I did, and with my husband, I truly felt alone. The good man in my life was gone.

My father's death left a loss so searing that a burning grief went with me everywhere I went. I felt that there would never again be a man as wonderful to me as he was, one who would love me as he had. I knew that my husband was not the man my father was, no matter how I tried to pretend he was.

By the time my father died, I had been married a little more than two years. My husband had hit me twice. I never dared to tell my father; it would have broken his heart.

My husband was kind at first after my father's death but grew impatient when I coughed at night and he couldn't sleep. I had asthma, and when I got immensely stressed or overtired, I coughed. I would lie in bed and cry alone; he had gone to sleep in the den on a pull-out couch. I was annoying, he said.

My asthma continued, and years later I learned it is common in abused women. My asthma started after we moved to Dallas, where a doctor told me that everyone's allergies are bad in Texas. I was given an inhaler and medications to control my breathing. I didn't relate it to the abuse that was killing me slowly, choking the life out of me every day.

Some people say to me, innocently, that for me to have become a victim of domestic violence, I must have been raised in a home with violence, that my father must have been abusive, that I learned to tolerate it at home. They suggest the impossible, just trying to understand. I don't blame them. I understand the question.

Still, I tell them the assumption is wrong, and that it is never that simple. I grew up with the image of a father and a husband as one with tireless respect and patience. I never heard him yell, and he would never have hurt my mother or even say something unkind.

My father was a gentleman. He held the door open for my mother everywhere they went, and he told her she was pretty. He told his children how much he cared for them. He showed us with examples as simple as ice-cream sodas on the hood. Once, when my brother Paul developed a high fever while my parents were out, my sister Mary Pat had called my parents at their dinner party, and they came rushing home. "I'm coming, Paul!" I heard my dad shout as he barged through the front screen door.

My father met my dates at the door and shook their hands. He read my stories in newspapers and magazines and beamed. Once he looked up from a story I wrote in *Chicago* magazine as an intern and smiled, "This is really good." I laughed at his jokes, and he laughed too, deeply and sincerely.

"Shaka-boom, shaka-boom, shaka-boom-boom-boom," he would dance in the second floor hallway of the house for no reason. He taught me to cha-cha, and he danced with me at my wedding to his favorite Duke Ellington song, "Satin Doll." He told me that he just wanted me to be happy. I thought I would be. I thought I had married a man like my father. An armadillo.

He was the kind of man who would balance six ice-cream sodas on the hood of his car and make it home safely. I had no other image of a husband or a father than one who was good and whole and safe.

A woman like me who has had a father like mine looks for the best in a man. A woman like me believes all husbands and fathers—all men—are like my father. A woman like me is so shocked by abuse that not only can she not comprehend it, but she denies it brashly. Cognitive dissonance erupts when reality doesn't fit into your program. You don't know how to process the information, so you pretend it isn't really happening. It can't be.

He didn't fit the stereotype.

I don't fit the stereotype.

You don't ask a rape victim if rape runs in her family. You don't ask a victim of a drive-by shooting if her mother was also the victim of a drive-by shooting. Violence doesn't always get passed down in families like blue eyes or a taste for chicken pad thai and beef with curry.

Sometimes there is no convenient excuse, no reason, no rationale. Sometimes there is not the simple explanation of a woman not knowing any better because her father was also a batterer. There are behaviors not neatly explained. The cycle must start somewhere. Sometimes you marry the violence, and it is totally brand-new.

I did not believe my husband was violent or dangerous because I didn't believe that could happen. Not to me, not to women with college educations—master's degrees even—parents who love each other, brothers who are kind, and work that is fulfilling. I didn't believe it was possible for me to be who I was, to come from where I did and to love a man who prayed for permission to kill me. The handsome man from the good family, the one with the parents who love each other and the father who reveres his mother, said he wanted to kill me. It didn't make sense.

So I learned to rationalize it by saying that if the person who loves you does hurt you, just don't let anyone know. Then it can't be true. Close your eyes.

Card received on January 17, 1995

Michele,

Thank you for all the love and effort that you give our family. I look forward to being able to work our relationship through the beautiful commitment you give as a matter of course.

We will have more fun and soon.

Love.

6

Masquerade

The oversized rubber butcher knife with the battery-powered lights in the handle was probably too much. But I bought it anyway. It was only $2.99 at a mall costume shop. The boys were a little confused when I told them it was for Mom and Dad's costume on Halloween. I wouldn't let the boys have toy guns in the house or weapons of any kind, so why did I buy a big knife for Dad?

My friend Jan invited us to a Halloween party, and costumes were required. It was 1994, four months after the brutal murders of Nicole Brown Simpson and Ron Goldman. I knew exactly who my husband and I should be for Halloween. I still can't believe I pulled it off.

It had been almost two years since the last outburst of physical violence at our house, and we had been going to see Father Gerry for counseling. My husband still made snide comments about my work or my post-baby weight, but I ignored him mostly and tried to be positive in Father Gerry's Saturday sessions.

"Aren't you proud of your wife?" our friend Dan asked once when he and his wife were out to dinner with us, discussing a recent column I wrote in the newspaper.

"For what?" my husband snapped.

Everyone at the table seemed embarrassed except him.

I confided about him in generalities to my closest friends. Every couple I knew had rough spots; my women friends all concurred with me that they had problems with their husbands. They didn't do this, they always did that. We mostly believed we were married to good men, though I never heard any friend say her husband hit her.

I told Jan once over lunch that sometimes my husband was mean.

"Do you think he has that seasonal disorder where you're in a bad mood because there's no sun?" she asked, innocently.

I didn't elaborate any more. I guessed my secret was too big to be understood.

My husband worked long hours. He had frustrations about his career, we had a large mortgage, the boys were small, loud, chaotic, and demanding. *It will all be better soon,* I thought. *It's a bumpy patch. Every couple has them.*

By the fall of 1994, the physical violence seemed to have receded, although I don't think I ever truly believed it was gone for good. Maybe I felt it had moved far enough away for me to publicly attempt to show who we both really were, who we had been. That Halloween it was as dangerous for me to masquerade as Nicole Brown Simpson as it was for him to wear O. J.'s jersey number. But we did. As deeply as I knew he was the same kind of duplicitous personality as O. J., I knew in the basement of my soul I was the same as Nicole: a battered wife. She and I had been in love with the idea of our husbands, the press release image.

It was my idea to be O. J. and Nicole; it was my leak of the truth to the world, a muffled call for help. Maybe because I felt the violence was no longer imminent, but in remission; maybe I felt safe enough to whisper the secret out loud. When you have hidden the truth for so long, you can never shout it out all at once. You must tell slowly, test the waters, take a peek first before you open the door all the way. You can't completely shed your disguise. Perhaps he complied with the masquerade because he wanted to show me who he really was, and show me that no one would believe it.

Violence aside, my husband was the perfect candidate to be O. J. He was as handsome, intelligent, charming, athletic, persuasive, and convincing as the rugged athlete whose name would later become synonymous with murder and spousal abuse. Both O. J. and my husband appeared to all the world to be ideal.

Though he had no Heisman Trophy, my husband was a college athlete, a boxer, a track star, a man who could use his body for triumph. A man who could use his body for harm.

I had met O. J. Simpson once, ten years before, at a press party thrown by an athletic shoe company during the National Sporting Goods Association convention in Chicago. When I was introduced to O. J., I saw how enticing his face was in its smooth allure, almost mesmerizing; he was so attractive and compelling. I remember later telling my women friends that his face was so perfect, chiseled, he was beyond handsome; he was beautiful. He didn't speak to me. He looked through me, smiling.

There were hundreds of people at the party, and O. J. was working; he was promoting a line of athletic shoes, working the room, the company man. I was also working, writing a brief about the party for *Footwear News,* the Fairchild paper for which I covered the convention, mentioning the celebrities who were there.

I even danced with O. J. He was a close friend of a man I knew who pushed us both to the dance floor during a fast song, and I was not about to be shy. I was going to dance with O. J. Simpson and tell every woman I knew about it the next day, although I don't think he even looked at me. My co-worker Dick, who was also at that party, kidded me for years about my dance with "The Juice."

I was dating the man who would be my husband at the time, but I went to this party without him. I was on a guest list, and I likely could not have gotten him into the private party, though I didn't try. I took a cab home to my apartment on Cedar Street after 2 A.M. There were nearly a dozen messages from the man who would be my husband, who would later masquerade as O. J. Simpson with me. But it was 1984. And I didn't know what I know now.

If I'd been told by a fortune teller what would happen ten years later to the man I danced with at a party and to the man I would marry, I wonder if I would ever have believed it. Both of these men were so handsome. Both of these men seemed perfect. If my life were a movie, the O. J. scene would be dramatic foreshadowing. I could not have fathomed I would receive the news of O. J. Simpson's acquittal in his criminal trial in 1995 as a weekly therapy client at a battered women's shelter. Little did I know that I would spend a Wednesday evening at Sarah's Inn discussing the horror at his proclaimed innocence with a dozen other women; all of us remarking on how uncanny it was that our husbands all reminded us of O. J.

For Jan's Halloween party, I bought a blond wig for myself and planned to wear a low-cut gold Lurex sweater embroidered with black bugle beads and a black leather skirt. I studied the photographs of Nicole Brown in newspapers and magazines and decided to scrap the wig and try to make my light brown hair resemble hers in style.

"It is macabre, sure, but it will be funny," I coaxed my husband.

I wanted him to wear a golf shirt and trousers. I bought him a black curly wig and brown face paint. He let me paint his face, but he wanted to carry a football and wear a jersey with O. J.'s number instead. He retreated to the basement to create the numbers on his jersey with masking tape. I dressed, carefully put on my makeup, and smeared ketchup all over my neck, throat, and hands.

I asked him to carry the butcher knife.

This is who he is, I thought. *Here is a man who batters, pretending to pretend he is a batterer, and it is all supposed to be a joke, a sick, tasteless joke. Will anyone see I'm not trying to be funny? Will anyone see who he really is? Will anyone look past my pretense and see what he has done to me? Will anyone ask? Will anyone wonder?*

Colin, who was not even one, and Brendan, who was four, started to cry when they saw me. It's just a game, I told them, and kissed them goodnight, leaving the baby-sitter to answer their questions about the pretend blood on Mommy's neck.

The reality behind the charade was too important to me to abandon. I needed to hint to the world: This is who my husband really is. He is like O. J. Simpson. He is a man who can kill his wife. And that is me.

At Jan and Kent's house, there was a witch or two, a baby, a farmer, a mermaid, a devil, and assorted predictable characters, some witty and entertaining. There was only one couple dressed as O. J. and Nicole. That was us. At first people thought I was a vampire, and then they moaned when I told them who I was pretending to be. Few said it was funny. And everyone said it was bad taste, even if it was timely.

You're missing the point. She and I are the same. My husband and O. J. are the same too.

In other years we had gone to parties dressed as other famous couples. In 1985, we went to a party in Dallas as Prince Charles and Lady Di. He wore enormous rubber ears, a tuxedo, and a red satin sash across his chest, with various pins and medals I had found in secondhand stores. I wore a simple silk dress and a hat. We won a prize. It's strange, now, to think I twice masqueraded as women who later died, who left their children behind.

The next year, 1986, we went to a party in San Antonio with his friend Greg and his wife, Lisa. We dressed as Sarah Ferguson and Prince Andrew. He wore pretty much the same costume, but without the ears. I wore a long green satin formal with towels and folded sweatpants used for hip padding, a red wig, and a tiara. I didn't know then that we had picked another ill-fated couple to imitate. A decade later we would be divorced, as would our Halloween alter-egos. But the year we were O. J. and Nicole was the most honest we had ever been publicly about who we were.

Nicole Brown's death haunted me. It was impossible to escape the brutal omnipresence of the murders and their details. Her death was a media obsession, and it reminded me that I could end the same. It was as if her death predicted my own.

Though she and I did not have the same lifestyle or attitudes, I understood her. She was married to a man who was a prince in all the photographs on the mantle and who was a tormentor in her own private hell. My husband and I were one couple in public, at the parties, in the photographs, at the family events, at 9:30 Mass at Saint Giles Church. Then we were another couple at our own house with the shouting, the cruelty, and the violence.

Could my husband kill me? My God, I didn't know.

At the grocery store checkout I would grab for the latest tabloid issue and scan for the stories on O. J. and Nicole—there were plenty—and read them before I came to the register. I couldn't buy one. I couldn't have her truth in my house.

One issue reprinted a letter Nicole had written to O. J. following a beating. She was apologizing and attempting to get back in his favor, eliciting intimacy and promising to get along with him, as if it was all her fault. I heard a psychologist on a talk show discussing this later, saying that apologies are common from battered women, who often do anything to try to make amends with their abusers, to stop the abuse.

On May 14, 1987, I gave my husband a card, following an argument when he had slapped me, the second time in our marriage. We had not been married a year. On the front of the card is a dreamy watercolor design with a quote from William Shakespeare: "The course of true love never did run smooth." Inside is printed, "I'm sorry." I added these words:

> *I love you very much, and I too, feel hollow inside and lost. But I feel we need to move from this and become closer. It's as if we are right up against it, the final confrontation, the questioning, the challenge of our souls.*
>
> *You frighten me and I frighten me because of the possibility of surrender. To love you completely means surrendering my guard and my fears and my inhibitions and the convenient reasons for not loving you completely. I miss you and our closeness. I feel saddened and betrayed, I mourn what has happened.*
>
> *The grief I know will pass and I think we should move to fill the holes*

with the wholeness we both need and require. Maybe it was necessary to have one huge conflagration to exorcise the evils and mistrust and fill each other with the entirety of an unfailing and unconditional commitment. I love you.

Mich

I was like her; I was like the other women I met at Sarah's Inn. We were all dancing around the truth, dressing it up, pretending the violence wasn't there. Not all of us ended up like Nicole Brown, thank God, but so many of us were damn close.

But that Halloween, I sat on his lap in Jan and Kent's living room, we made friends, we laughed, and we went home happy. Still, it was a different kind of night for me: I had let the truth escape, even if it was only a whisper, even if it was only enough to make people wonder. That night I was who I really was. With ketchup on my neck and a smile on my face, I was an abused wife. I was lucky, though, because unlike the woman whose persona I wore, I was only pretending to be dead. It was only Halloween.

Nine months after the party, before O. J. Simpson's trial and acquittal on criminal charges, I took photographs of myself in the mirror, my face swollen and distorted, the bruises violet and pale yellow on my cheeks, my eyes swollen and squinting. Finger marks on my cheek, four on one side, a thumb mark on the other. These were pictures not unlike the ones Nicole Brown had placed in a safety deposit box, which were later reprinted in most every newspaper across the country.

She and I were the same, but she was dead, and I was not.

Card received on March 29, 1993

Michele,

I really appreciate the effort you've made the past few weeks to make our marriage healthier. Yesterday was blissful to me. Spending the day as a family and as husband and wife.

The nadir that we reached last Christmas will be the beginning of an ascent beyond anything we've yet achieved.

I can't wait.

Love.

7

The Suitcase under the Bed

I folded the sweaters meticulously. Six cotton turtlenecks, sweatpants, something to wear to school, something to sleep in, socks, underwear, T-shirts. Nothing the children would miss, nothing he would notice gone. I packed a dozen diapers, size M, and baby wipes.

From the boys' shelves I took a handful of books—not their favorite Dr. Seuss books or the animal stories, but replaceable ones—and placed them between the colored layers of pants and sweatshirts, sizes XS, S, and M. Next to the diapers I put a pair of black leggings and a warm sweater—the brown one I never wear anymore—for me. Underpants. I could wear the same bra. Socks. We would wear our shoes. Anything more complicated, I could borrow. I didn't know where I was going, but I knew that I may have to go.

Beginning the last day of January 1995, I kept a packed suitcase under my bed. It was the large brown cloth and vinyl suitcase with the combination lock 345. That was the address of my first apartment, the one on Fullerton Parkway overlooking Lincoln Park, where I lived with Mariann in 1980.

The suitcase was blackened with use and worn from years of adventures, from three weeks in Italy with Mariann to business trips from Los Angeles and Santa Fe to New York, trips for fun to Florida, even our honeymoon in San Francisco. It was a big, reliable suitcase with wheels; one was missing, but it still rolled. For a trip years before I had tied a red ribbon around the handle. My father taught me that; you can spot it right away when it comes onto the turnstile. He was right.

The ribbon on the handle was frayed now, and when I finished packing, I zipped it closed and shoved it under my side of the bed. My husband was at work at the law firm on LaSalle Street, but packing made me feel nervous and fidgety, as if I had just betrayed him. As if I had told.

"Get a plan," said Mickey, the marriage counselor at the university where my husband had attended law school and where we had gone for counseling. "If he ever hurts you again, you have to take the children away." It was 1991 then, after the time my husband bit my arm. There were two little boys then; now, there were three: Weldon, Brendan, and Colin. Three blond little heads, six beautiful blue eyes. Six arms, six legs in the bright green bathtub each night. Bubbles in their hair.

Weldon was six and in kindergarten at Horace Mann School in Oak Park. Brendan had just turned four, attending preschool at First United Nursery School. Colin had just turned one, strong and bright, his eyes marbles of sky-colored blue. He and Brendan shared the same birthday, January 11. On Colin's first and Brendan's fourth birthdays, my husband was away on a business trip, a trial in upstate New York. He forgot their birthdays. He didn't call home for three days.

That had happened just weeks before, and the flowers he had sent to apologize for that were dead.

And he had hurt me again, this time on January 29, 1995. We were seeing Father Gerry this time, who handed me tissues as I spoke. No, he wouldn't be able to apologize anymore. Not for this.

"Please, God, let me kill her," he had said that night in January. Those words, his eyes not his own, someone else's. And after he had said those words, I had sat on the floor near the breakfast room, small and quiet in a corner, invisible, shuddering, and realizing that this would be the rest of my life.

I had papered the breakfast room walls white with crisp green ivy. I had put a colorful fruit border above the chair rail: pears, apples, grapes. Pears, apples, grapes. I watched them parade by from the corner where I shuddered. Pears, apples, grapes. The boys had peeled a piece of border from the wall over there. Pears, apples, grapes. Pears, apples, grapes.

The boys were asleep upstairs in their beds, as if nothing here could hurt them. Did they dream of Daddy praying to kill Mommy? Did they know? Did they hear me cry?

The next day I packed while my husband was at work. It seemed to help. See, I *did* listen to the counselor. I was making a plan.

I kept the suitcase under the bed, my treasure of freedom inside. He wouldn't find it, and if he did, he would never dream what it was for. Out-of-season clothes, I rehearsed telling him, though I doubted he would ever bother asking. I didn't matter that much to him. Did any of us matter that much to him? After all, he forgot the boys' birthdays.

The next time he gets angry, I will take the children and the suitcase, and I will leave, I plotted. *I will not tell him where, but I will go. What a damn shame Ellen, my closest friend, lives across the alley. Why couldn't she live somewhere he wouldn't think to look? I will just get in the car and go, to my sister Mary Pat's, my sister Madeleine's, my sister Maureen's. I can hide the car in their garages.*

The days passed and the rage subsided, as it always did, and then there were the flowers, as always, and the letters and the counseling sessions: January 30, February 6, 10, 13, 21, and 28. Emergency sessions, life-or-death sessions. It seemed the counselor's rule of thumb was that if you make a death threat to your wife, you must come five times a month. March 10, 24. April 17. May 8, 19, 26. June 9, 23.

"What do you need to happen before you can trust him again?" Father Gerry asked shortly after the January incident, when he had said those words.

"I need time to pass," I said, my voice deadpan.

I need him to be who he says he is.

The counselor understands, I thought. I wanted to shout to my husband, *Father Gerry—remember, you like him, you listen to him, he knows your family, and you talk about the old parish and the people you know in common. It's Father Gerry, and he told you, right there, I was right there, I heard him say it out loud, out loud, I heard it: "You brutalize your wife."* The words liberated me. *Someone understands. Maybe he can protect me.*

"You brutalize your wife."

It won't happen again. I am freed.

It was a game I played, pretending time erased the past. It was no more complicated, really, than telling myself my husband wasn't really abusive; he was just angry much of the time. It wasn't really about me; it was about him. *It's not my fault; I just have to stay out of the way. I just have to do everything right.*

"Please, God, let me kill her."

Sometimes the words would come back at me, regurgitated, as if they needed to explode from inside my memory. So toxic, my mind would not accept them. "Post-traumatic stress syndrome," Father Gerry said, and showed me the chapter in the book he had just read about it.

See, it's a real thing. Like war veterans. Like rape victims. I could be driving the children to school, and I would hear the words again, the thick, dark, death words, and I would feel a chill and a terror, and the only thing that calmed me was the suitcase under the bed.

It was enough to know it was there, under my side of the bed. The side of the bed he read the paper on, the side of the bed he watched TV from, the side of the bed he got hot and messed up and flattened, no matter how many times I asked him to move.

"You're psycho," he would say when I asked him to move back to his side of the bed, and I would wonder why it mattered so much that he not be on my side. I would take deep breaths and tell myself how silly it was that I was burned so deeply by him simply lying on my side, messing up the sheets before I got in them. How could I be so obsessed by his presence when I had made love to this man thousands of times? I would let his body inside me, yet I didn't want him on my side of the bed.

Then I would think about what was underneath. He was on my

side, hovering over my secret, dangerously close to discovering my plan.

I could have left anytime I wanted to. He worked early and late, every day of the week. Sometimes I imagined the children and I could be in Europe before he ever got home. I envisioned stealing away, like the Von Trapp family in *The Sound of Music.* He wouldn't know; he rarely knew what I did during my days, the stories I wrote, the victories I felt, the speeches I gave, the games the boys and I played, the pictures we drew, the love we felt, the tears that would not stop, the fear that filled me.

But I needed to think this through, all the way through. *I have three children now. I cannot be impulsive. This is not simple. He is not a boyfriend to dismiss. He is my husband. He is their father.* I prayed to my father, and I prayed to God, to Mary, to every saint I could evoke that I thought could hear me.

Help me know what to do. Help me keep my family safe.

Weeks passed with my secret hidden under the bed, giving me the strength to keep making his dinners and breakfasts, keep folding his clothes, keep dropping off his shirts at the laundry, keep picking him up at the train.

But the memories came back. I could log them neatly in my mind: New Year's Eve, 1986, Dallas. Hit in the chest. May 17, 1987, Dallas. We had an argument and he slapped me in our bedroom, among flowers and pillows. June 1988, Dallas, when I was five months pregnant with Weldon. In our duplex apartment, he hit me on the face. Spring break in March 1990, also in Dallas. Visiting our friends, a black eye. Then we danced and drank champagne. Weldon was one. October 1991, in the home we rented on White Oak Drive in South Bend, a few blocks away from the university law school. He bit me on the arm as Weldon, two, watched and I held Brendan, then nine months old, in my arms. I pushed him out the door into the cold fall evening and locked the door behind him. He banged on the doors and windows for me to let him back in. Weldon and Brendan were crying. Christmas Eve, 1992, in our new house on Linden Avenue in Oak Park, a suburb of Chicago. He was a first-year associate at the firm where my mother's cousin, a top partner, got him the interview and recommended him for the job. I had put up the tree just after Thanksgiving. The front hall smelled like pine; fallen pine needles lay on the floor. A swollen lip.

And then the recession, a break from the physical violence that lasted two years. He was getting better, I believed; the counseling was working. Colin was born. And just after Colin's first birthday and Brendan's fourth, the cycle came back. January 29, 1995. Even with a hiatus, it seemed too soon to even log it in. No matter how much time had passed without violence, more violence came. And I was never prepared.

"Please, God, let me kill her."

But I *was* taking care of it, I told myself; I *was* working to make the violence leave our house, leave our family forever. If the violence could leave for a while, couldn't it leave for good? I was solving the problem; I could make it change. If I tried hard enough to will the violence away, it would float away peacefully and be gone from my life, from all our lives, forever.

Some days I didn't even think about the suitcase, and some days I didn't even need to sit on top of the bed knowing it was only a few feet underneath me to feel calm. Some days I didn't think about leaving him and never being hurt again. Some days I forgot that he had said the word *kill.* Some days I didn't remember that he had acted violently. Some days he was good to me, and some days I even loved him.

And then it was my birthday, June 5, a warm and sunny day. I looked under the bed for something, and I remembered that all the clothes inside the suitcase were for the winter: the sweaters, the sweatpants, the pajamas with feet. I realized I needed to change them, and then I realized I had never needed the suitcase. Despite my fears, I never had to run away.

How foolish of me to be so drastic, so dramatic, I thought. It really will all be okay. *The handsome lawyer, the perfect husband, and the loving father is not really a violent man after all. Maybe he is all those fairy tale things I prayed him to be. Perhaps all the counseling worked, and see, no one had to know. How smart of me not to tell. I fixed it all.*

I envisioned sending Christmas cards for the next twenty years to all our counselors, who would smile and say to themselves that they knew we would make it, they knew the violence was just an aberration. We would be a success story! We would be the couple who had a glimpse of the nightmare, but who woke up. It was all a bad dream.

Of course it would be all right. How could it not? After all, we did have that weekend downtown at the hotel on Saint Clair for our seventh anniversary, and he had planned it all, a surprise for me because he loved me so much. He wanted to prove to me that he was a good man, a wonderful husband. He even asked his sister to watch the two boys; I was pregnant with Colin. We had dinner at a Thai restaurant and went back to the hotel where he was so aggressively passionate in his lovemaking. I was everything he ever dreamed, he said. He loved me beyond measure, he said.

If I concentrate on those memories, the bad memories will just be crowded out. There will not be a next time. I chose to believe him. I could talk myself into forgetting the past and concentrating on the future, the boys, our life as a family.

Still, some remote corner of my heart wouldn't let me unpack the suitcase. I supposed that even if there never was another episode of violence, I could give myself some insurance, just in case. Wouldn't it be great if I never needed it? Would I still be a battered wife if I still had an escape plan?

So I kept the suitcase packed under the bed. I decided that I would put in larger, warm weather clothes, and with every season that passed, I would celebrate the nightmare ending. I would celebrate never having to use the suitcase. I would celebrate that it was foolish of me to think he was violent, that he was really planning to kill me. I would celebrate that the man I married was safe. By now, I was very good at pretending.

I rationalized that I'd never need to cash this insurance policy, this suitcase under the bed. After all, if you have flood insurance on your house, it doesn't mean you are convinced there will be a flood, right? You have it just in case. If there was never another instance of violence, there simply would never be a need to use my suitcase. I would celebrate that I did not need to run away from my own home. I would put in larger size diapers for Colin and different books, and I would laugh that I had to keep this suitcase under the bed to feel sane, to feel safe.

The suitcase became a sacred symbol of the strength I had on hold, the part of me he couldn't convince, brainwash, or manipulate with his affection. It was the part of me he couldn't get to when I closed my eyes at each strike. Even if I acted as if I believed him, no matter how desperately I wanted to believe him, I knew enough somewhere inside to have an escape plan, a trapdoor, for the boys and me.

I wasn't really like all those other battered women on television, I told myself, because I was smart enough to have a suitcase under the bed. It was my reserve of power, the covenant of the only things I needed to keep my children safe. The suitcase became my silent, hidden protection, quiet and commanding. If anything else ever happened again, I was only one suitcase away from ending my encampment in a relationship that I had mistakenly thought was blessed.

Just one more time, I told myself, and I could get free. I needed just one more act of violence to prove who he is. And this suitcase will be my protection. And if I never needed to enlist its protection, then there would be a happy ending; my marriage was sacred, and my children were safe.

Then I am not a battered wife, and my husband is not a monster.

I felt a rising in me, a triumph. I hadn't needed my plan yet. The violence evaporated, I thought. *It's gone; it was a bad dream. He is who he says he is. He will never again brutalize his wife.*

One week later, over Father's Day weekend, he was going on a trip to Boston for business and for the wedding of a friend from college. I thought it was odd he was going alone and that he'd be gone on Father's Day.

You're a father, I wanted to remind him. *You have three little boys, remember? You've already missed their birthdays.*

He needed a suitcase, the large brown one. I let him search for it in the basement and watched him change, the anger starting to froth, the pacing, the impatience. He walked fast around the house in his white T-shirt, boxer shorts, black socks, and shoes. He never took off his shoes; they were hard and sharp and they hurt if he stepped on your bare toes—accidentally, of course. He said the storage area in the basement was a mess. He could never find anything he needed.

The children were asleep, Brendan and Weldon in the room I had painted with castles and a fire-breathing dragon. A peaceful place, with a dragon. Like our house. In our room, my husband was pulling out his freshly boxed, starched shirts from his closet, trying to pack but with nowhere to put his clothes.

"I know where the suitcase is," I told him, finally.

Crumpling, I insisted I was telling my secret not to the enemy but to my best friend. I told myself it was all right; he is my husband, after all; he is my friend.

"What are you talking about?" he snapped. "What?"

I explained and I cried and I pulled it out from under the bed. *This suitcase, this suitcase I packed just in case, and every time the boys get bigger and I don't need to use this, I feel better.*

"You're an idiot. That's crazy."

I emptied the suitcase. He went to Boston. That Saturday he missed Weldon's first home run on kindergarten T-ball. He was the youngest player on the Mets to hit the ball that far. We called him at his hotel to tell him, but he wasn't there.

I didn't leave a message.

Card received on April 9, 1992

Michele,

You have done a fantastic job with our finances and augmenting our income with your freelance work. I don't know how you do it, but I know I married the best a man can marry.

Love.

8

Pawnshops, Discover Card, and His Checking Account

I was writing checks on a dismal February morning in 1995, paying the bills in my bimonthly ritual. It was a Friday, his payday, and I had gotten into the convenient habit of calling the bank's automated checking balance service to see what checks were cashed and how much money was in the account.

For the previous three years, he'd had an automatic deposit service through his law firm, placing his fortnightly paycheck into our joint account. By early Friday morning of every other week, the money from his firm was neatly deposited into our joint family account, the one we opened the day we bought our house on Linden Avenue in Oak Park. We also got a clock radio from that bank, the one at the end of our block whose digital time and temperature billboard could be seen from most every window of our house.

I dialed in the PIN number and listened for the automated robot voice to dispense the balance information. There was less than $100 in the account. There had been no deposit that day. It's only 10 A.M., I thought, I'll try again later.

I wrote the checks and set them in a pile on my desk in the makeshift office I shared with Colin. In one half of the room was his crib and his baker's rack—painted white and filled with stuffed animals—and a watercolor painting of the cow jumping over the moon. In the other half was my desk blocking the glass door that went out onto the roof of the family room so the boys couldn't unlock the door and go out there. I separated Colin's area from mine with a four-paneled screen my husband had made for me. I painted it turquoise with gold suns and silver moons. Brendan and Weldon painted the stars.

I put stamps on all the bill envelopes and positioned the return address stickers neatly in the left corners. I did not mail them. I called the bank service a few hours later, but the balance remained the same: "ninety-seven dollars and fifty-three cents," the voice chanted, in the same lifeless timbre as it might say "nine thousand dollars" or "nine million dollars" *There must be a mistake with the payroll department. It will be fixed.* I forgot about it.

I took Weldon, then six, to afternoon kindergarten and changed a half dozen diapers on Colin before I thought about it again. I left a voice-mail message for my husband at work. He didn't call back.

The next morning at breakfast, I was feeding Colin in his high chair. Bits of pancakes enlarged and soggy with maple syrup dotted the floor, and orange juice pooled in quarter-sized splotches on the bright pear placemats, blue and orange.

"Could you check with payroll? There was a mistake and your check was not deposited," I said as I passed him in the kitchen; he was hovering over the sports page, standing near the sink.

He did not answer me.

"We have no money in the checking account, and I have to pay the bills," I said more forcefully. Maybe he hadn't heard. Brendan and Weldon were watching cartoons in the family room, the volume turned up high.

"We're not using that bank anymore," he said without expression or emotion. "I got a new account downtown." That was all. He didn't look at me.

I could barely breathe. Panicking, I picked up Colin from his wooden high chair, washed his face at the sink, and told him to play in the family room with his brothers. My husband had moved to the breakfast room. I followed him.

"What account? Show me!" I was furious, scared. *This is it. Now he is like the men in the movies. Another betrayal. Another blow.*

I followed him as he walked upstairs, my neck sweating underneath my hair. From his maple dresser drawer—the dresser that had been my father's—he produced a folder from the new bank. I grabbed it from him. He had opened an individual account in his name only, with his name on the checks and the printed address and phone number of his office. He had not even used his home address.

"This is not the checkbook of a married man with a family," I shouted. My hands were shaking. Benign familial tremor, Dr. Carlson called it when I went to see her in November. "Are you under a lot of stress?" she had asked. Is a violent husband stressful? I had wanted to ask, but of course didn't.

Even when doctors raise suspicion, we don't let them know. We all say we fell. We all blame refrigerators or sharp edges. My pediatrician later told me she dismissed my fat lip and black eye when I brought the children in for shots or ear infections because I said the boys had thrown toys. Still, she wondered.

I could feel the blood rushing out of my head, ten thousand thoughts competing for my attention, all of them screeching his betrayal. I was pacing, holding the checkbook in my hand, glancing again and again at it to see what I had missed. Where was I? Where were the boys? Where was a father? A husband? He had checked the box indicating it was an individual account. He checked the box giving no one else access. He had used his office address as if he lived there, as if he had no home here. He had denied his family three times.

"Where will I get the money for groceries? Where will I get the money for the baby-sitter?" I was screaming, crying. I felt trapped. "What are we going to do? What have you done?"

Though I was freelancing for the *Chicago Tribune* and had a one-year single project contract with a large advertising agency, most all of my money went to baby-sitters. I cursed myself for depositing my last quarterly $2,500 paycheck from the advertising agency into our joint account, the practice we had held for all of our marriage. *I paid the monthly installment on his damn law school loans with that money,* I thought. *That money would have lasted the boys and I for months.*

"When would you tell me? When I bounced a dozen checks? When did you make this decision? Why didn't you tell me?"

He was calm. He said he opened the account the day before. Later he told me that he had to inform the law firm payroll two weeks earlier to stop the automatic deposits. He told me to put the groceries on Visa. He told me I didn't need any cash. He told me it was time he took control.

"I will handle all the money from now on," he said, walking over to his desk in the corner of our bedroom. He was authoritative and distant.

I walked back and forth, room to room, confused, dizzy, half listening for the boys downstairs. Were they all right? Did they know what he just did?

My panic was mushrooming. How would I pay for Brendan's preschool? What if I needed cash and wasn't paid for thirty, sixty, or ninety days for my articles? I called my friend Ellen. I didn't care if he heard. This was too big to hide. This meant I was really powerless.

"Calm down," she said. "Didn't your mother give you money to buy a used car?"

Yes. My mother had given me $10,000 to buy a used Volvo station wagon from the used car dealer in Michigan where I'd had my previous cars serviced. The money she gave me was in the savings account, the account I did not have access to on the cash station card, the account he did not have access to on the cash station card. I had taken the money out of the checking account just a week before so it could earn interest. It was taking longer than I thought to find the right car.

"Relax. You have money. You and the boys can live. Were you planning on spending $10,000 this weekend?" She made me laugh. "Have him fix this. Tell him you can't live like that." I hung up and finally could breathe.

He took all the money away. And he never said a word. What else could he do?

I walked downstairs. We were standing in the dining room, the one I had painted turquoise the year before; underneath the first coat of paint I had painted our initials as an adolescent gesture of affection.

"You tell the bank to change this account to a joint account with my name on it. I can take money out anytime, and I can write checks. You do that Monday morning."

He agreed but said he would write all the checks from now on. He said it was something his mother told him to do to keep me in line. I didn't believe him. She wouldn't do this to me, not to her grandsons.

"Are you planning to get a divorce?" I asked him. I could not feel my hands or legs. I no longer trusted him and knew I could not predict him.

"No, I am doing this for us. We need to save money."

After I could stop pacing and the panic was in remission, I tried some of the marriage counselor's tricks. Assume the other person is benevolent and has your best interests in mind. I went through the mental motions, although that was an assumption I could no longer make.

In counseling a few days later, Father Gerry handed me a tissue while I told the story.

"No more new hurts," Father Gerry told him. After all, it had only been a few weeks since he prayed to God to kill me. "No fresh wounds," Father Gerry reminded him. "She needs time to recover."

If I had told my mother, who had given us money during law school to live on, the cash to buy our last two cars, a 30 percent down payment on our first house, and had eliminated our credit card debt, she would have been furious. Madeleine and my mother had given us every piece of furniture we had in our house, except his desk, two Queen Anne chairs, an armoire we bought used, and a dresser he had from his first apartment. Oh, she would have been mad. She would have not forgiven him for taking her generosity and betraying me, betraying her trust.

So I didn't tell. On top of all the conflict, I didn't want to deal with her hating him. After all, she thought he was charming. She loved him like a son. If I fix this, she will never have to know.

A week later Brendan's preschool tuition was due. My husband told me that Brendan should not be in preschool and that it would be cheaper to have him stay home. He told me not to pay it and see what happens. The tuition per month was only slightly more than the monthly payment and dues at the health club my husband went to every morning.

I had a baby-sitter twenty hours a week and used every minute of that time to write and work. All my freelance checks went to paying her. In order for me to make more money, I needed full-time help, which we could not afford.

It was difficult enough finding a part-time baby-sitter twenty hours a week for three boys under six. No one lasted very long, and most of them quit after a few months. Celia quit after the first day, and I had thought it was a good day. Diapers, tantrums, and three active, willful boys were more than anyone cared to deal with three—or more—days a week. Some of them laughed when I said I needed light housework done too. "How do you expect someone to get anything done with three boys?"

Exactly.

Okay, I told myself. *I can work this out. I know I can come up with ways to get cash.*

I looked through my jewelry box. *I really don't wear jewelry except for my wedding ring and earrings. Look, here are the gold chains my father gave me and I never wear, and here are the pearls I haven't worn since our wedding.* I concocted this fantasy that my father wanted me to sell the chains. Fumbling through the jewelry boxes, I talked to him as if he were in the room.

"Please help me, Dad. I need help. You are pulling me out of this, you are helping Brendan, you are giving me solutions again. I don't need a gold necklace."

There was a strange comfort in that; I felt his presence, and I imagined him condoning all of this. Helping me, yes, my Dad was helping me.

Over the next few days I looked through the Yellow Pages and talked to a dozen people on the phone who ran ads for estate jewelry. Most did not take gold chains, and many were completely uninterested in the strands of pearls that had been mine since adolescence.

I called one pawnshop in Oak Park and talked to a man who said he would look at the gold chains and give me a fair price. He was affable and kind on the phone. Don't bother with the pearls, he said.

See, everything will be all right.

When the sitter arrived, I took the gold chains (including one my father had bought me in Greece) and placed them in a red silk jewelry bag my mother had brought me from a trip to China.

I parked the car on the street and walked to the front entrance of the pawnshop on Harlem Avenue, off Randolph Street, hoping no one I knew would drive by and see me. I felt ashamed. A shabby patchwork rabbit fur coat dyed different colors was hanging on a hook behind the counter. Outside it was raining.

I was nervous as I rang the bell. The man came out from behind the black bars in the back.

I explained that I had called about the gold chains. Carefully I opened the red silk pouch, untying the white cords and laying before him the three gold chains. "These were from my father," I said, my voice and hands trembling.

He took a few minutes to eye the chains and to eye me.

"I will give you $70 for all of these," he said.

I told him again they were from my father—perhaps he hadn't heard—and that they were very thick and special gold chains. He stared at me, unmoved.

"Okay," I said. He counted out three $20 bills and a single $10 bill. He laid it on the counter.

He scooped up the chains and as he ripped them apart, breaking the links, he said, "This is what I think of your father and his special chains. We melt it all down." Then he looked at me and said, "If your father worked harder, you wouldn't be here."

I almost choked on my tears. What did he know of my father? What did he know about how hard he worked and how much he loved me? This was not about my father; this was about the man I married, the man I thought *he* was.

That morning I opened the door and ran out into the rain, the bell above the door ringing behind me. Gasping for breath, I sat in the car and sobbed.

"Look what you made me do," I shouted to the air, to my husband who was miles away in his office at the law firm with pictures of our children on his desk. "But thank you for being there with me, Dad, thank you, Dad, thank you, Dad," I said over and over, the only mantra that could calm me.

It was several minutes before I could drive.

And when I did, I brought home an emptiness so severe and a hurt so sharp I prayed that my husband would come home late that night so I could silence this vicious, infected secret and not have him know what he had done to me.

Now all I needed was $60 more to pay the tuition. I took the rest out of the savings account for the car and said nothing, hoping the cost of the car would not exceed what was left.

A few days later, I still could not look my husband in the eye. But he was my best friend, I told myself, and if he knew how upset I was, he would be aghast and mournful and sorry for what he had done.

I still believed he was a man who did not want to hurt me, a man who loved me as much as he said he did in all his letters and all his toasts and all his public tributes. I was quite sure that he would hold me and apologize and say he had made a mistake, that taking all the money out of our account was cruel. Then he would be a good father and a good husband, and I would never be afraid again.

So I told.

We were in the family room when I told him; he was watching television, and I had just finished folding the day's three loads of laundry and placing them in white and blue baskets, separating the whites, the colors, and Colin's clothes washed in Dreft. He did not flinch; I was shaking. He glanced at me briefly and said, "Thank you for telling me," and went back to watching television.

My eyes were filled with tears so thick I couldn't see if he was smiling.

The next day I told Ellen on the phone. The hurt felt new and fresh, just in admitting the words.

"Look what he's done to you. Don't ever let anyone do that to you again," she said. "Don't you have a Discover card in your name?"

"Yes."

"You need money, you get a cash advance. You pay it back as you can. Don't ever sell anything of your father's again. If you need money, you work it out together. Never let him do that to you again. He is required to provide for you and the boys."

In the weeks and months that paraded past, the hurt became more distant as I tried to push it beyond me, past us. I tried not to cringe when he talked about the lunches he had out or what he did at the health club. I charged the groceries. I made speeches at women's clubs and was paid by check on the spot. I kept the money for the baby-sitter and things the boys and I needed like shoes, presents for birthday parties, or trips out for cheeseburgers to placate them.

I lived with a vile tumor of resentment, growing and gnawing. He reduced me to selling my father's gold chains. This was not an ironic twist on O. Henry's "Gift of the Magi." This was a sorrowful, hurtful, sadistic way to denigrate another person. *This is how much he respects me.*

I lived between the betrayals, trying to hide what I needed and acting as if nothing was wrong. I cried in the shower at night with the water running to muffle the sounds of the pain that haunted me. I tried to quiet the voice inside me telling me he was not the man I thought. This would not be okay, and this story would not have a happy ending. He lied to the marriage counselor, and he lied in his toasts. To me he was a vicious, controlling, abusive man. Even if no one else could see.

But to admit and act upon that would send me into a towering, consuming uncertainty I did not want for myself or my boys.

So I played the game. I lived on denial and cash advances from Discover card, knowing there was a limit, knowing that eventually this too would have to end.

Card received on Christmas, 1992

Michele,

This is a crossroads for us. Once we pass this we will come to a deeper under-standing and appreciation of who we are as a couple and as individuals.

Christmas is a difficult time in that it presupposes Christ will be born again in our lives. It seems as though we need to bring the little child of God back into our relationship.

I commit to you again, as I always will. I wish us a deeper love and an abiding faith in each other for 1993.

Love.

9

The Power to Change Him

When she finally found out, my mother had a hard time adjusting to my truth. It's not that she didn't believe or support me; it was that she was dumbfounded. And when you are a mother and your child is hurt, you search for answers and any solutions you could have offered, signs you could have processed so this would not have happened, so your child's pain could have been avoided. Even when your child has a cold, you ask yourself, *Should I have made him wear a hat? Did I leave the window open? Did I not care for him well enough?*

I imagine a mother who loves her daughter—as my mother loves me—is constantly second-guessing herself as to how and why her own daughter could be hurt and she could not know. Knowing that the model for marriage in her house was not like this, how could I have become a victim? My husband wrote her letters, too, and toasted her at parties. The deception was thorough and pointed. Each kindness eclipsed the cyclical acts of abuse.

My mom could not understand how this wonderful boy, her close friends' son, could act violently and how I could stay. My father was not violent. My husband's father was not violent. She could not swallow that she had been fooled, that I was hurt and she didn't know to help me. Where did it come from? Why did it happen to her daughter?

So she talked about it with her friends, trying to get a handle on what happened, trying to picture her youngest daughter in the same boat as women on the news, women without families like ours, women whose stories of horror and assault were so horrible they seemed surreal. I remember watching a television news piece about a woman whose partner set her on fire. Was I like her? My story was dissected and passed around parties more often than Brie in puff pastry served with water crackers.

My mother returned home from one Saturday afternoon luncheon to call and tell me the support I was receiving from every woman who heard that I had been abused and that I was alone raising our three little boys. She then recounted a story of a friend who said she couldn't believe I had such low self-esteem I would allow myself to be hit. She had been reading my columns and stories for years in the *Chicago Tribune*. She said she thought I thought more of myself. I seemed so confident.

Common wisdom holds that if you are a victim of domestic violence and are hit by a partner, then you must feel pretty bad about yourself. Your self-esteem is in the toilet. Once you like yourself, you will know you don't deserve it. And you will leave. It should be simple. What's wrong with you?

This is not the whole story.

I always knew I did not deserve it. I was not trying to be punished for something, to make restitution for an imagined or assumed sin. I was not making up for some perceived lack. I knew intellectually that the violence that harmed me was not about me. My error in judgment was that I believed I had the power to change the man I loved and to make the violence disappear. I assumed the responsibility for our marriage and believed I was powerful enough to make it work. I believed I could make a man who acted violently into a man like my father. I had the answers. I could perform the magic, saving him, saving me, saving all of us. *Ta-daa!*

I saw him as very bright, athletic, witty, and ambitious. I thought if only he saw himself the way I did, there would be no more problems. I correctly believed that self-esteem was part of the equation of domestic violence, but I thought it was all his part. I believed that if I built him up and helped him see his potential, then he would love himself, me, and the children fully and wholly and without violence. The way a father and a husband should. The way my father did. The way my husband's father did. The way his brothers did.

I did not possess a haughty savior complex. This was a belief system developed from and supported by the culture I lived in, the relationship books I'd read, the talk shows I'd seen, and the counseling sessions I'd had with my husband for almost a dozen years. I believed that if I was happy with myself, gave him the space to be happy with himself, and was truly good to him, then the violence would dissipate like an ether cloud. *Poof.* We would all live happily ever after, pretending it never had happened.

It was my plan. It was what I hoped would happen, what I needed to happen. And in the lapses of time where there was no violence, the months when he was loving and kind, acquiescent and compassionate, I made myself believe that the violence had disintegrated, that my plan had worked. I had changed him into the perfect husband, the kind of man who would dress up as O. J. Simpson just to humor me. He truly revered me for who I was; he saw me for me. The bad dream had ended.

I knew I had the power to change him. Love was powerful, and I loved him more than I thought was possible. But my love for him was a love based on endurance, struggle, delayed gratification, and excuses. The highs were great and seemed long-term. He said they were. The lows were shackled to their own excuses and explanations. What lay in between, the white space between the episodes, was fine.

"Give a rat unpredictable, intermittent reinforcement, and it will run in circles all day long," a friend told me. And the rat was me.

The first time my husband hit me, he blamed his actions on the tense first year of marriage. Just wait until after our first anniversary and it will be better, he said. We have details to work on, issues to iron out, the counselor said. Sometimes he drove fast and recklessly to the counselor's office, making me think we would never make it there, or back. But on our first anniversary we went to dinner in a limousine, a prize for a dance contest we won. *It's over,* I thought. *The nightmare just happened twice.*

The next time my husband hit me he blamed his job, worrying about finances, and feeling unhappy about himself. Even his excuses were not about me. He never said he hit me for anything I did. He always said it was his fault, at least to the counselors.

The time he hit me when I was pregnant, he said it was because he was panicked about being a father, anxious about money. The times after that, when he either struck me or was raging, he dismissed because he was stressed about the LSAT exam, then going on vacation with Weldon as a baby, then not doing well enough on the LSAT, then worrying about getting into a good law school, then worrying about doing well at law school. Other incidents occurred because he *was* doing well in law school—and he needed to keep doing well. Then it was the stress of two small boys, law loans, and our lack of money.

When he got a job at a prestigious law firm, he was worried if we could get out of debt fast enough. Then he raged because he hated Christmas. Then he became furious because we went for a long winter weekend with his family in Wisconsin. He was periodically upset about money or work or the boys. He hit me on the Fourth of July weekend in 1995 because I told him I didn't like the way he made jokes about me.

Each time he cried, "Mea culpa!" I believed he was a man who was flawed in his approach to anger, but a man with good raw material nonetheless. He was a man from a good family, a man who knew the violence was his fault. He said all the right words, and I wanted so hard to believe he was not a violent man. I talked myself into accepting all his chest-pounding apologies.

I can't fully explain why the repetitive behavior wasn't enough on its own and why his shallow excuses could distort the importance of the violence and revoke the impact of each strike. I can't explain why I wasn't willing to see the big picture. I only know he looked good in the family photographs, beaming next to me as I held the little boys' pink hands, their miniature bodies warm and safe in my lap. It was as if I was always trying to convince myself that this man was truly good and that I just needed to put the proper spin on his actions.

He taught Sunday school. He mentored a young African American high school student without a father. He changed flat tires for strangers on the expressway. He visited the elderly in housing projects. He volunteered his time. He was the golden boy at work. He changed the oil in our cars and scrubbed the front hall carpet when it was dirty. He wrote long letters. He called from the office and told me he loved me. He said how much he wanted me. He cried when he said he never wanted to be alone. When he would whisper to the boys, "The best gift I can give to you is love for your mother," I would feel true relief. I never pictured how true the converse would be.

Until the seconds before a strike, I could not predict when the abuse was coming, and I was surprised every time. Even the last time in July 1995, when I spent the day taking photographs of the boys—beaming in brightly colored shirts—for our family Christmas cards. If you had told me that morning that today my life would change forever, I likely would have laughed out loud. The photo I took that day is framed in the family room, the boys' faces beautiful and innocent, a reminder to me of the last day I lived in blindness.

Many times the abuse was near an important celebration, like Christmas, Mother's Day, or a birthday, but there was even a time when one of his sisters was having a large party in South Bend. I guess he bit me two days before as a test to see whether I would put on a show for a crowd and act happily married right after. I canceled with his sister instead, making up an excuse that the sitter couldn't come. She told me how much she wanted us to be there and offered some other sitters' names. He begged me to go.

We went to the counselor's office the following day, and he was so remorseful that I wore long sleeves and went to the party. He told me he prayed for help. He even said a decade of "Hail Marys" in the car on the way to the party.

After the counseling sessions following each act of abuse, there was a healing period, and each time I convinced myself he had changed. To admit that he was a cyclical batterer meant that I was forever the abused wife. I couldn't see myself that way. I wouldn't see myself that way.

"I am a good man," he would say to me, sometimes in tears.

I believed he was—or could be—a man who put his family above everything else, a man who would love me forever, a man who cherished me and supported me. He wrote all those letters. I believed he was a man like my father, a man like his own father, who kissed his wife and played with the grandchildren and meant it.

I believed the cards my husband sent, because I wanted to so badly. And when he came home from work with flowers or with a new dress for me, I felt he understood me and cared for me, nurtured me. I felt he knew my worth, his own worth, and that the violence was gone. I felt he owned his behavior, took responsibility for his actions, and was accountable.

After all, he was capable of being a good husband for stretches at a time. "I don't deserve her," he would tell my women friends. On the playground at Mann School, where Weldon was in kindergarten, another mother told me about the dinner for the Sunday school volunteers a few days earlier, where he proclaimed what a great wife I was. She was surprised I didn't react more excitedly. So she told me the story again.

I never knew if those stretches of restitution would last or how long the bouts of contrition would hold. I had to stay busy looking ahead. It was too horrible to look back. It was part of my blindness, but also part of my irrational attempt to convince myself this was as good a man as my father. With my father gone, he had to be.

I stayed because I didn't understand how you could walk away from someone you had once loved. I could not understand how you could be present in a hospital labor and delivery room with a person and later say you didn't love him anymore. How can it be so temporary? Love demands permanence. It was black and white. If you love, you stay. Like an obedient dog at the foot of the bed. Like people committed to each other.

I believed life held certain constants, like the sun rising and the waves hitting the shore and staying married and in love forever. I believed that once you were married, you solved any problems that arose.

But at that time, when we were married, I had never known problems without solutions. I had never known that giving up was an option. I was born into privilege and expected a life without adversity or tremendous challenge. Life was a simple equation of cause and effect. The cause of his anger was his own, and I would help him stop it.

I was brought up in an Irish Catholic community where divorce was nonexistent or extremely rare. When I married my husband, I thought that no matter what complications arose, we would always be together. I couldn't comprehend that a marriage could end. Only on television soap operas did anyone really say, "I don't love you anymore," and move on to the next partner, serial brides and grooms. In my mind love was not something that stopped. But I wasn't able to see or admit that this wasn't love. This was abuse.

The conviction of forever love comes from my Catholic upbringing and the concept that love from God is never-ending. The love I received from my parents and my brothers and sisters was unconditional. When you get married, I thought, your spouse becomes your family. And your family loves you forever.

After my husband was gone from the house and before he filed for divorce, we had a telephone conversation about finances. He was still charging on our Visa card, and he withdrew the $700 in the checking account reserved for the boys and me to live on.

"Get money from your family," he told me brashly on the phone.

"You *are* my family," I said to him, crying.

"No, I'm not."

It's hard for me to remember precisely now, with all the treachery and anger and hurt, how it felt to love him so deeply and why I envisioned him as I did, when all the signs were screaming for me to get away. It was illogical to assign him good intentions. It was absurd to keep trudging to counselor's offices after each incident of abuse and to keep believing that each time he hit me was the last.

Now, I can't remember what it felt like to love him. That part of my heart's history is eradicated, stolen, as if I never loved him. But I have a memory of professing love for him. I know I felt so much pride in everything he accomplished. And I also remember thinking that every time he did something outstanding—became a law school's law review editor, had an article published, graduated cum laude, won a case, gave a momentous opening speech at a trial, or wrote a brief that was acclaimed—I felt a relief. *Now, he will finally feel good about himself and be the man I want him to be. He can relax. I can relax.*

The better he felt about himself, the safer I was. So it was in my best interest to keep him happy and to provide the playing field for him to succeed. Would I get up every night—without asking him—to feed and change a crying baby, to soothe a sick child? Yes. Would I have dinner ready every night, make sure he had minimal involvement with chores and drudgery? Yes. Would I have celebration dinners for him, throw birthday parties, and buy him gifts for his successes? Yes. If he loves himself, he will love us all.

I went to a federal courtroom one day in 1993 to hear his opening speech of a trial. It was a big case he had been working on for months as a young associate. He was involved in the trial with two partners at the firm. His cousin Matt, an attorney at another firm, came to hear him too. I was very proud of him.

I had helped him with the speech, and it was good. The words were carefully chosen, and he had practiced it dozens of times. He was extremely nervous, though, and mostly read from his notes without looking up.

On L.A. Law, I thought, *no one reads the notes; they just speak.*

At the end of his oration, an attorney sitting near Matt and me turned to his friend and said, "That was about the worst opening I have ever heard. He was so nervous; it was awful."

I looked at Matt and without speaking agreed that was a comment we would never repeat. When it was over, my husband came back to us, and I was effusive about how great he was, how proud I was of him. One of the partners said his wife doesn't come to his opening statements and it was remarkable that I did, especially with my work and the boys being so small. But I did it, so he could be happy. So we could be happy. I would never have told him someone thought he was terrible.

When you love someone, you want them to succeed, to be the best person they can be. I loved my husband that way. As time passed, it became clear to me he did not love me the same. Perhaps he did not love me at all. Perhaps I could not love him enough to change him and to change his mind. Perhaps what I did didn't matter at all.

The books and articles were wrong. All the fix-it prose, the relationship books as numerous as fad diet books, should come with a disclaimer: "If your partner is violent, none of this will work." From what I have read, some women who are abused feel that they deserve the poor treatment. But not all of us. I thought I was powerful enough to change him. I knew I didn't deserve it. I thought I was so powerful I could make him love me well.

The women that I met at the weekly meetings at Sarah's Inn were nurses and administrative assistants, businesswomen, college graduates. None of us signed up to be abused. None of us fell into the stereotype. I later learned there are so many of us, so many millions of women who are battered, that a single type is impossible. Not one of us at the shelter stayed because we didn't like ourselves. We said we had the power to change him—whoever he was.

I knew the violence wasn't about me, but the violence was to me. I separated the man from his actions and the actions from myself. If he didn't mean to hit me, then he didn't hit me. If I didn't feel I deserved it, it wasn't as bad as it looked. Even if it was me bleeding, even if it was me with the bruises. Even if it was me crying so hard at night that I couldn't breathe. If I was unwilling, did that still make me a victim?

Maybe no one has the power to change someone else. Maybe the power is in leaving.

I thought I was strong enough to stay. But after twelve years with a man I loved, I learned that a man who batters cannot be changed. A man who behaves violently has to change himself. I was ashamed that I had been hit. But I was also proud that I had tried everything I could. All the power in the world could not change this man. I took back my power and used it to get away.

PART TWO

GETTING OUT

Card received on Christmas, 1990

My dear Michele,

You have made this Christmas so special for me and my family. You have worked through the isolation of being in South Bend and have made this time beneficial to yourself, Weldon and me. You now will bless our family again with Brendan. The commitment you have made to give our children the most loving attention and care possible is more than I could have asked. It gives me a peace about their future that I would never have had. The commitment you have made to me and making law school the most for me has allowed me to excel beyond my own expectations.

You do inspire me, Michele, the way you work through these initial rejections of a book. Your mental toughness of writing right after a rejection has taught me a lesson I could only have learned from witnessing your tenacity. The trials you are enduring will bear fruit, maybe even beyond your own expectations. We both have prayed for your literary success. It will happen. When it does, we will celebrate so richly.

We have a little more than a year left in South Bend. I am just beginning to see the strain you have been under. I have law school and its countless associations, but you have only Weldon. I almost cried when you said you have to go buy something to have a conversation. On the other hand, the isolation has taught us to better care for each other. We have learned to appreciate what we do have, you and I. For all my blocking tendencies, I have learned to listen to what you ask of me. However long that might have been in coming, I am happy you have gotten through to me.

Finally, my love, I want you to know that our love grows each year. I feel the love others have for you. I feel Madeleine's love for you, your mother's and your father's. I find myself talking to him, in conversations I did not initiate—about how you are doing and how I could help you. With all those who love you working so hard for you, you must truly feel blessed this Christmas.
Love.

10

We Are Family

When Colin, my youngest son, was three, he had a most endearing approach to justice. If you put his toys away before he was finished, perhaps accidentally stepped on his toes, ate a potato chip from his plate without permission, or violated his sense of propriety in any way, he would stand with his hands on his hips—all thirty pounds of him—pout his lips exaggeratedly, and shout, "You hurt me!"

He could be consoled immediately with a hug and an "I'm sorry." Then he would march off, reabsorbed into his world, acknowledged and comforted by the logic of simple cause and effect, the offense forgotten, forgiven. There was no malingering, grudges, or withheld acknowledgment of his hurt.

That's all I wanted too. I wanted to shout to my husband from the top of the stairs, "You hurt me!" And I wanted it to be over, done, an apology delivered that was heartfelt, a hug that guaranteed it would never happen again. A guarantee that I could believe.

The last time he hit me, part of me ached for reconciliation, but another, stampeding part of me was drowning that wish and pushing me to action. Still, damn it, he could have tried.

It was July 4, 1995, and it was raining. We were in Towers Lake, Wisconsin, and I had been holding out since he hit me for the last time on the night of July 1. The night I screamed and his mother and father had come into the room.

The night I had told.

That final night, three days earlier, I had sat on the floor, dabbing my mouth with the washcloth filled with ice cubes his mother had given me. Amid the cacophony and confusion, there was an eerie, distant clarity about what I needed to do. He was talking fast and loud and pacing.

"I'm married to *that!*" he shouted, pointing to me, as if it was a defense.

I remember his mother and father talking, his father loud and upset. His father hugged me and told his son he was wrong, and that of course, you never, ever hit your wife. You never, ever hit a woman. I could see the hurt in his father's eyes, the disappointment so severe it was almost palpable. In the minutes and hours that followed, there were so many words said and so many explanations offered, all I could do was shut out the blurring, whirling noise of voices and click off the plans in my head:

Number One: I would not call the police in Wisconsin.

Number Two: I would deal with it in Chicago, in Illinois.

Number Three: I would get home and I would call my sisters. It would all be over.

And then I reentered, attending again to the dance of voices, and listened to his mother as she told me to call my own mother, her friend, the next morning.

"I can't tell her now," I said. I did not want to worry about how the news would affect her. She would be hurt; she would be scared.

"If it means anything, he is sorry," his mother said, apologizing for him.

"It doesn't," I said flatly.

Banging, empty words bumped around me, around us, as if we were sitting in one giant pinball machine for what felt like hours. His mother tried to mediate and told him there was no excuse. His father said he was ashamed. Still, his mother asked what I did to make him mad. His father told me it takes two to make an argument.

Yes, but it takes one former boxer to almost break your jaw.

And then I got up, went into the bathroom, and threw up. There

112

was blood in the toilet as it flushed, red ribbon streams circling the shiny white bowl. The boys were still sleeping. His parents were still talking. The windows were closed because that night was unusually cool. His father went out the back door that led to the beach and stood on the porch, smoking a cigarette. I never went back into that bedroom. I stayed near the back door for a moment, and his father walked back in. As I cried, he gave me another hug. For a second it felt like I was hugging my own father. A strong, loving father.

I turned back to the house, walked quietly into his parents' room, and reached into the crib where Colin was sleeping. I picked him up and carried him into the room where Weldon and Brendan were sleeping in bunk beds, curled like croissants under the blue covers. "Bump beds" Weldon called them, because you bump your head if you get up from the bottom bunk too fast.

I placed Colin down on the other bed pushed near the wall, with the brown checkered pillowcases. I pushed a dresser in front of the door to keep my husband out. I needed to be safe from him. I needed to plan.

Then I laid in bed, holding Colin on my chest. But I could not sleep. I had to make my strategy. I would stay at his parents' house as long as I could stand it. The boys loved it there, and I would not perform a dramatic exodus with them crying and confused. I would plan, not be impulsive, think this through. I refused to add another painful memory to their lives, one of me prying them away from their father, away from the grandparents whose company and affection they craved, away from the house that meant only joy to them. I knew what I was doing would be irrevocable. I had to be sure.

What compelled me to finally act was the abysmal realization that this was what my life would always be like. Why it had taken me so long to realize that, I don't know for certain, but I knew there was no going back. I knew more certainly than I even knew my name that for the rest of my life there would be periods of calm, then, whenever, wherever, for whatever reason, an eruption of violence, violence so wholly unpredictable my husband could sit in a marriage counselor's office one day and then throw me against a wall in his parents' home a few days later. There would always be this threat, even with the weekends away and the flowers and the cards and the boys who had his berry-blue eyes. And the promises that there would be no more.

I was thirty-seven, and I realized for the first time that for the next forty years I would be strapped to a cycle I wanted no part of, that I had no control over. His cycle.

In Father Gerry's office a few days before, we had talked about how great the weekend in Wisconsin would be, and we had talked about my recovery from the last episode in January, the time he prayed to kill me. We had talked about another episode in April, when he became so angry I told him the next time I would take the children away and leave him. That time he sat on Weldon's bed and cried, "I don't want to be alone. I don't want to end up alone." The session had seemed to go well.

He had seemed so sincere to Father Gerry. We had laughed on the drive to his parents' house, I-290 to Route 53, followed by twists and turns on Wisconsin roads he knew so well. I made bruschetta for his brother's party. I made chocolate chip cookies. I brought strawberry coffee cake. I packed the bathing suits and the diapers, the sunscreen and the small red sandals. I packed for myself a straw hat, a black bathing suit, and a cute sundress for the barbecue party at his brother's summer house. I packed red, white, and blue clothes for the boys. I packed hope.

But now, swollen and scared, with Colin in my arms, I felt strangely whole. Colin's smell, the softness of his skin, his white-blond hair brushing against my neck—all these were reasons I could no longer allow a man who hit me in their lives, in our lives, in my life. He was no longer making sense; he could no longer explain himself. No cards could make up for this. I would not have my children raised in a house that was not safe. I would not let my little boys grow up to be violent.

The sons of violent men are seven hundred times more likely to be violent, I remembered from a story I wrote. *My boys will not treat a woman the way he treats me.*

I was doing this for them, as much as for me. It is better to have no father in the house at all than to have one who acted violently. The world did not need three more violent men.

I vowed to pack our bags in the morning and wait as long as I could before demanding that we go. The boys could go fishing, swimming, paddle boating. They could collect rocks, chase frogs, and grill hot dogs with their grandfather. They could play with their cousins, the boys with the same blond hair and the same sense of urgency, the same cadence in their run. Because this would be the last time—for a long, long time and maybe forever—that they would come to this house.

Suddenly he pushed the door open, shoving the dresser back. He said in a low voice how stupid it was to put furniture in front of the door.

"What are you going to do?" he asked.

I wasn't sure if he meant today, tonight, or forever.

"I will let you know," I replied. "Stay away from me tomorrow, go to the library, do not touch me, do not talk to me." He had a legal brief he needed to work on. I would be safe. *If he is gone from the house, I can think. I won't feel the hate I feel for him now.*

He left the room, and I didn't bother to move the dresser back. Nothing could stop him anyway.

That next day was Sunday. Brendan, who was four, woke up and stared at me on the next bed. "Did Daddy hit you?" he asked.

That brief question from that small voice, his blue eyes wide and wet, cemented my purpose. He asked it as blankly as if he had asked if it was raining or if we were having pancakes for breakfast. For the first time I did not lie to him or to any of the boys. "Yes."

I knew what I had to do.

All day I avoided my husband's brothers and my sisters-in-law when they came to the house. I stayed in the back room, putting Colin to bed for a nap, changing his diaper, acting busy. I avoided my friend from Chicago, a woman I volunteered with on a hospital board, whose family had the house next door as their summer home. I felt shy and ashamed. I was hiding. His mother was kind, and she took her son to church with her in the morning. I stayed behind.

"Call your mother," she told me again as she left. I didn't.

His father volunteered to drive me back to Oak Park in my gray Volvo and to bring my car back to Wisconsin for his son to return at the end of the weekend. I said no, it was my car, and I couldn't be trapped in Oak Park with the kids without a car. "I'm leaving with the car when I need to, and he can figure out a way to get home," I told him. *For God's sake, let him take the train,* I thought. His father seemed surprised at my response.

I stayed there in that house, in the home where he hit me, the home with the wreaths that I had made for the bedrooms, the home with the "Welcome to the Lake" sign I bought for the door. I stayed in the home that I first visited twelve years before.

But I busied myself as I always did, playing with the boys and ignoring my husband. I said little to his parents, who acted kind but embarrassed, as if the worst thing to say would be that their son was violent. I'd had enough talk anyway.

I felt I could no longer straddle the line between what I knew to be true and what I wanted to be true. There was an ambivalence I could no longer hold at bay, keeping everything in check, making sure I did not bleed my secret in public. It was out now. I could no longer pretend he did not hit me. I could no longer pretend I was not who I was, a battered woman, a beaten wife. My husband abused me.

Nothing prepared me for the blazing shock of this admission. Nothing was as frightening as saying it out loud. *My husband is still beating his wife.*

My mouth had two dozen or so lacerations on the inside, marks for each tooth when he slammed my jaw with his fist. There was a grapefruit-sized bruise on my arm and a softball-sized lump on my head where I had hit the wall.

The cuts in my mouth made eating nearly impossible. They were open sores, tender, and they stung when food hit them. I could not brush my teeth without squealing. But the boys and I went swimming and adventuring on the paddleboat. I wore sunglasses to hide the tears dripping out of me, as if there was so much hurt inside it overflowed. I stayed Sunday and then Monday night. We went to his brother's party, the house on the lake with the hill and the deck and the speedboat. I put lipstick on my swollen lips. They looked as if I had implants.

At night, he slept in the other bedroom, where he had hit me. I slept with my boys in the room with the bunk beds and the wooden dresser and the night-light the boys demanded stay on always.

On Tuesday, July 4, it was raining early. Just after breakfast, I announced that we were leaving. I told my husband to get his things together and that he should take the two older boys to a movie when we got home. I needed to unpack and think.

His parents hugged me long and hard. I didn't tell them what I planned. His mother told me she loved me. His father told me the same. They kissed the boys good-bye, and as we pulled away, his mother looked small and fragile from the driveway. His father looked pensive, concerned. It wasn't their fault. It was his. I knew they were confused and hurt, but I also knew they loved their son. I couldn't blame them.

Still they were there, they saw what he did, they heard what he said. It was not as if it was anyone's version of what happened. I didn't imagine that it would be nearly three months before they spoke to me again.

We drove home the way we always did, the same route his father took that night twelve years earlier when he told his mother he could not live without me. But today Colin was in his baby seat, Weldon was in the middle seat, and Brendan was sprawled out way in the back, in the third seat, where he held court with his dinosaurs and his Batman figures.

I couldn't look at him, barely even in his direction. I did not dare let on what I would do. Because now I was afraid of what he could do to me. I was afraid of what he could do to the boys. I wanted to get home, safely. I imagined him swerving off the road, like the men in the movies, the violent ones you need to be afraid of. I did need to be afraid of him, and I was. My fear tightened around me like a straitjacket.

There is an eclipse when you are changing your life's stance, a darkness as your past slides by your future. All you can hope for is that the light will emerge so you will see again. You're not sure it will, yet, because this time is so dark and so painful. Everything about me hurt. My body, my heart, my thoughts. It was a hurt that had been squashed for so long it erupted and left me unable to speak.

For our entire relationship, I had been recklessly positive and forgiving, seeking solutions, trying to work around him, trying to offer better answers. I was trying to pretend that the good times and the kindnesses expressed who he really was. The volunteering, the gestures, the letters to my mother. But even looking at him differently couldn't change who he really was. He was the only component in my life that I couldn't make better, that I couldn't change. There was no positive spin for this.

Here is where earnest love absolutely did not count. And for the first time, I was realizing that no matter what I did, he would always hurt me.

For the first time, I could see him as a man who was so puzzling that I could never know him. This was not just a man I could jokingly call "Eeyore" because he saw rain clouds in a blue sky. None of this could ever be funny. Or simple.

This rage of his, this rage I could not control, was so unpredictable and so powerful, that when I thought of him I had to strain to remember loving him. To me, he was a stranger, a malevolent stranger. He was a man who would hurt me, who could hurt my children, who was truly terrifying because the violence came on his schedule, without warning.

"I guess these rhinos are more dangerous than white rhinos, because the black rhino will attack for no apparent reason," he later wrote in a card to Brendan, one with a photo of a black rhino on the front. I wonder if he saw the similarities.

I did, and that realization was exhausting and enervating at the same time. When I looked ahead, I could not see where the violence would end. But I could no longer look back. I knew that much. And as we drove, I could not look at him.

We got home and I started to unpack and do laundry. It was about noon, and I picked up the newspaper outside on the front porch. I looked up show times and theaters for movies.

"Take the boys to the movies," I said. "I want to go to my sister Maureen's house for a family party. I will take Colin. You drop the boys off when the movie is over and come home and work. Do not come to Maureen's; I will say you have work to do." He missed a lot of family parties because he had work to do. He missed a lot of our lives because he had work to do. I couldn't stand the thought of my family feeding and entertaining the man who had done this to me.

Besides, I was going to tell.

He was amenable and conciliatory, but he always was after an outburst of violence. This pattern I was used to. The boys were happy to go to the movie and happier still to go to a party when it was over.

I called my sister Maureen and told her we left Wisconsin early, that Colin and I were coming to her party, and that the other two boys would be there later. I almost told her on the phone, the tears falling as soon as I heard her voice. But I waited.

He left with the boys, and I called the Sarah's Inn hot-line number. It was a local hot line I had called anonymously in January, when he had threatened to kill me. I had given donations to Sarah's Inn; a friend of mine was on the board of directors. Months

119

before, when my friend asked if my husband and I wanted to go to the annual fund-raiser, I said no, but had to laugh to myself. *If you only knew.*

I told the woman on the phone what had happened, and she told me I needed to go to domestic violence court in Maywood and get an emergency order of protection, but it was not open today—it was Independence Day. How fitting. She said I did not need an attorney and that an advocate from the shelter could go with me. She told me what hours they were open and gave me directions. She told me to go in the morning and asked if I needed a place to stay tonight.

No, thank you.

I would not let on to him. He would never imagine I would do this. He would never imagine that I would tell and that I would act. He thought I would be too proud to parade my humiliation. *You should not hit your wife,* I said to no one there. *And you should not hit me. Your mistake was hitting your wife. Your mistake was hitting me.* Sometime long ago he forgot I was strong.

I placed Colin in the car seat and drove the few blocks to Maureen's house. My sister Mary Pat was in the driveway. "What happened to your face?"

I told her. She held me and picked up Colin and said she would do whatever I needed her to do. Her husband, Ken, a veteran Chicago police officer, overheard the story, walked up to us, and put his arms around me. I asked him whether I should have reported it in Wisconsin. He told me that if I had, I would have had all the follow-up court dates in Wisconsin and that I could report it in Illinois.

"Get the physical evidence," he told me. "Take pictures. Get a doctor's report."

Mary Pat went inside to call our sister Madeleine, an attorney, who was at her own summer house in Michigan. I told Maureen, and she held me. "Everything will be fine. Oh, Mich," she said, sounding like my dad.

My husband came to Maureen's a few hours later with the boys and stayed for dinner, filling his plate with a cheeseburger, potato salad, coleslaw. He grinned all during dessert. I could not look at him and kept motioning him to leave. He stayed. The sight of him now made my stomach tighten. To look at him and feel his arrogance, his assumed immunity, made me physically ill. To me he seemed as bold as a murderer who stays in his victim's house to eat a meal. Cocksure, invincible. My sisters gave him dirty looks.

That night he acted as if nothing had happened and came upstairs to get into our bed.

"You are not sleeping here. There is a consequence," I told him. He slept on the living-room sofa, the one I had recovered in blue and white striped linen slipcovers.

That night Mary Pat called me. "I told Madeleine. She is taking care of everything. She is getting you a lawyer. She will call you tomorrow. Don't tell him a damn thing. Are you safe?" I told her that I was, though I wasn't really sure of that or of anything.

I tried to brush my teeth, but the lacerations made that too painful. Hearing me cry in the bathroom, Weldon called to me from his bedroom. "Are you okay, Mommy?"

"Mommy hurt?" Colin called from his crib. Now here's a family conversation to record.

He left for work the next morning, as usual, expecting me to make breakfast, I think.

Madeleine called shortly after 8 A.M. from her office. Her physician husband, Mike, would come over that night and write a report on my injuries, she said. I was afraid to go to the emergency room; I did not want the boys to witness that trauma. I didn't let them watch police shows or *America's Most Wanted,* and I wasn't about to let them live through an episode starring their mother. My part-time baby-sitter, Maria, was on vacation for two weeks, and I would have had no choice but to take them to the hospital with me. Instead, Mike came over when the boys were asleep and measured my bruises. I couldn't help but cry.

"Oh, Mich," he said, with tears in his eyes.

But I had the strength to take a picture of my face. It was swollen with a hand mark in blue and brown covering the left side. I shot the photograph with my arms outstretched in front of me and dropped off the roll of film at the one-hour photo store. The rest of the roll of film was of the boys playing at their grandparents' summer house in Wisconsin. I had taken no pictures on that roll of him.

I asked my friend Ellen to pick up the pictures and to keep the photograph of me in the envelope. I didn't want to look at myself. Not yet.

"Show me the pictures of the boys," I asked instead.

The next few days were a blur. I could not sleep. If I laid down, I would cry, as if when I relaxed, all the pain would leak from me.

When he was at work, I could breathe, but I still could not rest. There were so many details to prepare, as if I were planning a funeral. I was burying the past, burying the violence, but in a public ceremony, not the way I had buried it all along with my excuses.

Madeleine suggested I work with an attorney at her firm, Bob, a man whose son played with Brendan. It would be best for him to handle my case, she said, because he already knew me and it wouldn't be as scary. Bob called me several times over the next few days to ask me questions for the affidavit he was preparing. When I said out loud all the incidents of violence, repeating dates and times, it was overwhelming. I had never added them all up.

But seen together, added all together in rows of print as I wrote them out on a lined legal pad, it was suddenly obvious my husband was more than a man who occasionally lost his temper because of stress. This was the pattern of a cyclical batterer, a man who would find a way to vent his anger at me, no matter where we lived, no matter what year. The dates were moving closer together: January 29, 1995; July 1, 1995. Five months. It was the shortest gap and the most severe of all the incidents. I could see, now that it was on paper, that the gap would eventually close in on me. I imagined it would keep closing, the slices of freedom growing smaller and more narrow, until there was no more me.

Card received on July 23, 1993

Michele,

Another back-dated document from your attorney-husband. You do light up my life. I know you think you're last on my to-do list, when it comes to birthdays and anniversaries, but it's not the case. I am so proud of our seven years. We are beginning to love each other in ways we both knew we could attain. Our love is growing and will continue to, dear God with us. I love you, Weldon, Brendan, and our baby to be.

Love.

11

It Was Crowded

We were scheduled to go to domestic violence court at 11 A.M., Friday, July 7. I would tell the judge what had happened, with Bob, my attorney, asking me questions. Bob had gone over the routine with me on the phone. I was only to answer his questions and not elaborate. I would get an emergency order of protection for three weeks, twenty-one days. It would be over by noon.

I could hold on for three weeks. I still did not want to end my life with my husband. I just wanted to end my life with violence. I wanted him to get help, to enroll in a violence program for men, and to be magically pronounced cured. I did not want him back in our house until he was better. I still thought he could get better. I wanted him to hurry up and come back before school started, before September, so nobody would know. Since he worked most of the time anyway, I could explain his absence all summer, and nobody would know what had really happened.

The ambivalence was choking me. I wanted the monster gone, but I wanted the man he pretended to be to return. I said I could hang on by myself for one year.

For three nights before I went to domestic violence court, he slept in our house, eating dinner in the kitchen hours after the boys and I had finished. He talked about small things, minutiae, but I couldn't hear him, as if the volume were turned down and all I could see were his lips moving. As if I were deaf.

I avoided his eyes; I avoided him. And each night he came upstairs to get into our bed, and each night I told him to sleep downstairs.

On Friday morning, after he left for work, my sister Maureen drove me to Madeleine's office downtown. I don't remember how we got there; the expressway was a blur, the details whirring past. I was glad I was not driving. I could not concentrate. I had felt this in labor with each of the boys, a pain so consuming it was impossible to focus. Breathing was a chore. All I could do was surrender and stop fighting the feeling, to do what needed to be done.

The pain in my acknowledgment that my husband perennially abused me was so much, so intense, I couldn't contain it or escape it. This was pain that touched every cell of my body. This was pain that was not overshadowed by the elation you know you will feel when a baby is born; there would be no happy end to this day.

I hurt also because I felt betrayed and foolish. *I guess he never did love me. I guess it would always be this way. I guess he lied. You can't love a person you hurt. I have three children with a man who doesn't love me. I have spent one-third of my life with a man who would rather strike me than hold me. I was completely fooled. What's wrong with me?*

When we got to her office, Madeleine brought me a Diet Coke, and Bob showed me the documents, including the affidavit of abuse, which I signed. The affidavit cited the times since 1986 that he had hit me and where. Seeing them typed neatly made me gasp. There were so many. While reading some old letters, I realized I had forgotten at least one. There were probably more. But I had refused to remember.

We walked over to the State of Illinois building on Randolph Street near Dearborn, which housed the domestic violence court. I could not hear the traffic. Madeleine held her arm around my waist. Maureen carried my purse. Bob was quiet. I could hear my shoes clicking on the pavement. My legs felt like rubber legs, Gumby legs. I had worried about what to wear, like defendants do in the lawyer shows on television. *Have the witness wear something nice to look credible.* I picked a white blouse and a tan skirt, long. A black blazer. My face was still swollen. I wore little makeup and small gold earrings. I didn't look like me. It wasn't my face.

We walked into the building housing the domestic violence court, and it was crowded. I was shocked. To know what it meant to be there, to know what it took to admit, what pain was endured, and to see so many women waiting—scores, hundreds of women—was disturbing. To realize that what had happened to me was not only horrible but also common was hard to absorb. Had we all spent the Fourth of July terrified?

It was as if we were waiting in line for the movies, there were so many women there, with their children, some in strollers, some in car seats, some so small they slept on their mother's shoulders like kittens. Some children were crying.

Sign in. Take a number. Wait your turn. Dry your tears. Next.

When you are suddenly in a place you never imagined you would be, everything around you becomes exaggerated, like a hallucination, and you struggle to remember details in the blur—the color of the carpet, the color of the wood on the wall, what other people are wearing—as if in the details lies the sanity.

Madeleine did not let go of me.

We waited in line, the five of us. A summer intern from the law firm came with us; she had typed up the documents and she was concerned. She told me I looked pretty. I felt as if I was choking.

As I looked at the women with me, with us, I felt compassion and empathy. "I'm sorry for your hurt," I wanted to tell them all. "I'm sorry for you. I'm sorry we're here."

Like them, I waited my turn, waited until my name—my married name—was called, as if we were waiting in line at the bakery or for the pediatrician. It was so crowded.

The woman in line before me was a beautiful, raven-haired young Latina; I guessed her to be less than twenty-one. Her hair was curly and fell to the middle of her back. She wore a white blouse and slim black pants. She was alone. She told the judge through tears about her husband, who grabbed her by her hair and then pushed her out of his car, still holding her hair, dragging her from a moving vehicle. As she told her story, I started to cry.

This is me. I am the same. We are here telling our stories, our impossible stories of men who loved us, of men who hurt us. We are no different.

The clerk called my name. Madeleine and Bob walked with me to the judge's bench, and Bob identified himself as my attorney. Madeleine identified herself as an attorney, acting in an unofficial capacity, and also as my sister. She was holding me up, her arm around my waist. I was afraid if she let go, I would fall down.

My body was shaking. It was not something I could control, this shaking from the inside, these tremors I could not understand or stop. I could speak no louder than a low whisper; the words were too horrible to say out loud and my mouth was still swollen. Judge Cunningham leaned over and looked sympathetic, asking me to speak louder. I answered Bob's questions. Then the clerk asked me to take the gum out of my mouth.

"I don't have gum in my mouth," I said.

I glanced at the court reporter, who wiped her eyes, filling with tears. The clerk apologized.

The judge then stopped the proceeding and began to describe what my face looked like for the record. He described the swelling. Later Bob told me that the judge's inclusion of his observations on the record were quite important. My injuries were in the court record and could not be denied.

I only felt ashamed.

In what felt like an hour or two but was only a matter of minutes, I was granted an emergency order of protection. I remembered the judge asking me if my husband had somewhere to stay. I said his family lived in the area. It was just after 11:30. Only half the day had passed, and I had changed my life.

The court reporter smiled at me as I left and told me kindly to take care of myself. I felt like a ghost, without a body, without a face. The clerk called the next name on the list. The line coiled around down the hall.

Back at the law firm, Bob called my husband at his office to tell him there was an emergency order of protection for myself and the children forbidding him from going into our home for twenty-one days. Bob asked him if he wanted courtesy service of the order away from his office. He said no.

Bob asked him about visitation, and my husband said that he would not be seeing the boys for a while. He needed time. Bob then asked him if he would like to come into the house for an hour when the boys and I would be gone to pack his things and pick up his car. He said no, have me pack his bags, have me put them in our second Volvo and park it in front of the house. He then recited a list to Bob of things he wanted, down to his gym bag and his dental floss.

"I'm not packing for him," I shouted when Bob told me.

It was better this way, Bob said, now he's not in the house, now you don't have to worry. It will be all right. Pack his stuff, then you don't have to deal with him.

I was angry I was still doing his work. As dutifully as if I were picking up his shirts from the cleaners, I was packing for him to leave his family, because he'd made it impossible for him to stay. I made the choice for him to leave, but he'd made the choice to hit me again. It was my choice to make it the last time.

The letter Bob wrote to him accompanying the documents stated that divorce was not my intention. I wanted that to be clear. I wanted him to know that all I wanted was for the violence to stop. I asked Bob if the affidavit listing all the abuses could be left out. "He'll be so angry if he knows I told about all of them." I was crying.

Bob was incredulous, looking at me as if I had just asked him whether we had to admit we lived on Earth. "Michele, this is the point. He has to know you told. You were here to get the order of protection. He has to have all the documents." We had an appointment that night with the marriage counselor, I told Bob. Did he think I should cancel it? Bob looked at me, dumbfounded.

"You're not going to the appointment tonight," he said. "It's too late." I guess he couldn't believe I didn't know the answer, but what I had done had not yet sunk in. I no longer was supposed to try. It was all over.

Maureen drove me home. Madeleine went to my mother's office to tell her what happened. My mother came over immediately and told me how sorry she was, and how she wished I had told her. She was shocked, she cried, she said she should have known.

We ordered dinner that night from New Fue City—chicken lo mein, egg foo yung, egg rolls—just as he and I had ordered together for years. It was the same menu we'd had on the two New Year's Eves I was pregnant with Brendan and Colin, the nights we had no money to go anywhere, the nights when carryout Chinese and a rented movie were all we had. I wondered what he was eating, if he was eating. Later my friend Carol told me she had seen him out that night at an Italian restaurant downtown with a large group of people. He was laughing. There were men and women there, a group of about ten. For God's sake, he was celebrating.

I gave the boys a bath in the bright green tub on the second floor of the house we bought together on Linden Avenue. He had caulked the tub in neat, bright white snakes of caulking. He had placed new screens on the windows. Overhead was the new fan he had installed. My head was pounding. I had already taken ten Tylenol that day, and I still hurt. My jaw was stiff and aching. My chest, my heart, my arms hurt. It hurt to think.

It was easier to be hit once in a while, I said to myself as I crawled onto the couch after my mother had gone home and the boys were in bed. The thought haunted me, popping up like closed captioning. *I know it's better for all of us, but this is much worse than a black eye or a fat lip. Exposing your nightmare is worse than living it all.* When you have been used to living in blindness, having the lights turned on—bright like searchlights—makes it hard to focus, hard to see. You know it is better this way, but the light still hurts your eyes.

Before they went to sleep, I told the boys their father was on a business trip. I had told so many lies about him already it was hard to stop. I couldn't answer my own questions; I couldn't answer theirs too. I needed a night off from their pain.

About nine that night, after the boys were in bed, my husband came to the front of the house and drove away in the maroon 1985 Volvo my mother had bought for us when we lived in South Bend, the car I had packed. I slipped a note in one of his suitcases. It read: "I had to do this. The boys need you." I didn't say I loved him because I really didn't know if it mattered. But I did sign it, "Love, Michele."

I don't know if he ever read it. I only now know that when he pulled away from the curb that night, he was never planning on coming back, he was never planning on getting help and getting better. He filed for divorce a few weeks later, something he must have been contemplating immediately. Getting a divorce is not like ordering drive-through fast food. It takes time—weeks, sometimes months or years. He might have had it planned all along.

He was never coming home.

Ellen came over from across the alley, bringing me a glass of wine already poured. We cried together and she held me. "You did the right thing," she said and hugged me.

Numb and in cool disbelief, I prayed she was right.

Card received on September 7, 1987

Mr. Bookies to his Lovey Buttons

Dear Lovey,

Driving in our car from Hot Springs, after our unplanned but heartfelt second honeymoon, makes the tardiness of the card slightly more acceptable.

I feel such a kindred spirit with you that we are from the same family. And we are now, because we have become one together.

I love you so much. You are teaching me that our love can take care of each other in a healthy way. For the first time in my life I know what I need and I have someone to answer those needs. How God has blessed us.

I love you with all my heart and soul.

12

$18,000 and the 1987 Porsche

There should be such a thing as divorce insurance. After you become engaged, you call your insurance agent—the one who handles your home, car, fire, and flood policies—to apply for an accidental divorce policy, a rider like dismemberment or accidental death. Just a little extra insurance to make you feel safer on your honeymoon.

Describing the emotional and physical health of your intended to your agent, you can also receive discounts for a nonsmoker, a nondrinker, a college graduate professional who lived with his mother until marriage. The policy would cost about $150 a month, and you pay into it as long as you are married—it doesn't even have to be happily—and you can cash it in as soon as you become separated—five, ten, fifteen, twenty, twenty-five years later—to put a down payment on your divorce attorney's fees. If you stay blissfully married and never get divorced, you can also cash out with a tidy little sum to go on a cruise around the world with the partner you will love forever.

This seems perfectly logical to me now. Divorce insurance is as necessary as medical insurance because the cost of a divorce is as high as having triple bypass surgery followed by a month-long stay in intensive care. Neither of which you would have planned for when you were young and in love. If you can pay for a heart attack down the road, why shouldn't you be able to begin payments prenuptially for an attack on the heart, eventual alienation of affection?

On the day we were set to reappear in domestic violence court for a renewal of the order of protection on July 28, 1995, three weeks after it was first filed, my husband filed for divorce. The documents were logged in at 11:00 A.M. in a separate building; our appearance in domestic violence court was scheduled for 11:30. It was a clever legal move, Bob told me. The judge in domestic violence court would have little patience for him as an abuser and would tend to be more compassionate and lenient toward me, granting me more of what I needed, especially since the children were given to me in temporary full custody. My husband would never allow himself to be in that position, Bob suggested. He wanted to be in control.

With the filing for divorce, the case would be merged into one file, it would be considered a divorce case, and I would be given no special treatment. In divorce court, Bob told me, it was open season on everybody. The judges try to be fair and split it all down the middle. There is no prejudice from the domestic violence.

Now I had a divorce attorney too, and the judge later ordered the children be assigned a guardian ad lightem—their own attorney representing their needs—because my husband would not agree to much of anything I requested.

So every month my divorce attorney and the children's attorney sent me Monopoly-money bills, with $100 charges for telephone conversations asking—and likely not even answering—one question. The total bill for the divorce could have bought a Porsche or two. A few Volvo station wagons. Definitely some trips to Disneyland, maybe braces, new shoes for all the boys all through high school, and then a second car. A home office.

I spent nearly the equivalent of three college educations (okay, at state schools) for my children on hearings, motions, pleadings, mediations, complaints, violations, and attempted settlements. And I am still spending. I thought once the divorce was over there would be no more legal battles. I was wrong.

If only I had thought to invent divorce insurance when he asked me to marry him, I would not be borrowing and paying—in installments for the rest of my life—to sever and keep severed ties with a man I once loved deeply, a man who hurt me, a man who is still fighting with me.

The financial hardship is not even the most distressing. Divorce is so painfully and inextricably tied to immense personal hurt that just entering the Richard J. Daley Center on Clark and Dearborn streets would make me feel as battered and dejected as a night after he hit me.

"This is a place where everyone thinks the worst of the other person, and the whole point is to hurt the other," David, my second divorce attorney, once told me. Bob, my first attorney, who thought his involvement would be briefly confined to a simple emergency order of protection, handed over the case three months later to David, whose practice was solely divorce. And months after the divorce was final and the legal bills kept accumulating because of visitation and child support disputes, Bob came back on the case at a reduced rate simply because I could no longer afford to pay the steep costs of a high-profile divorce attorney. A friendly divorce is an oxymoron. An expensive, painful divorce is all that is possible.

The divorce courtrooms at the Daley building in Chicago are filled with men in shiny suits—some middle-aged, some impossibly young—and harried, dark-suited lawyers gripping bulging black leather satchels of manila folders and papers. The women attorneys are dressed in navy, brown, or black and carry huge briefcases while the women clients try not to look as if they are dying inside. Everyone is a caricature.

On every bench, in almost every chair, it seems, is a woman— older, younger, beautiful, tired-looking, well-dressed, hastily dressed, inappropriately dressed—who looks horrified. The men look tired, some defensive. Others look defiant and laugh and smile, whispering to their lawyers. The despair is practically contagious.

There was so much sadness and so much pain in each courtroom and each hallway, which fermented with case-numbered people on Thursday mornings at 9:30. Here were couples who could no longer stand within reach of each other without severe animosity. And here was me. I would look down, doodle notes, and write down descriptions of every person in the room to distract myself from what I was feeling. I would write lyrics of songs and words to prayers just so I could crowd out the hurt that was building exponentially inside my body just by sitting in that courtroom.

Just sitting in the hallway on the sleek chrome benches, waiting for his name to be called, would make me want to cry. Most of the time it was all I could do not to. The sound of clicking heels on the floor, echoes of whispers, sharp words said hastily.

I could never look at him straight on, my almost-ex-husband. He made a point of smiling and joking with his attorneys—he had two different attorneys before representing himself, then going back to his second attorney, then hiring a third—and made an effort to look not only pleased with himself, but deliriously victorious. His first attorney was a bulldog of a woman who made comments to Bob about my husband "biffing" me and how difficult it was to control the boys, who deserved to get "whacked" now and then.

His second attorney was a bulbous-nosed older man with red cheeks and a balloon belly that hung over his pants and made the buttoning of his frayed suit jacket an impossibility. His third attorney was younger and more polished but seemed genuinely surprised when my attorney mentioned something in the file that had happened before he was on the case. He said he didn't know the case began in domestic violence court. Is that why there were two case numbers in the file? Is that why the case was consolidated?

I felt so heavy, laden with dread, in that hallway, in that courtroom, crowded with women and men alienated and cruel to each other, that I needed to sit because I could not bear the weight of my hurt without support. I would walk in the ladies' room to breathe and wash my hands and pretend just for a minute that I was anywhere else, in the ladies' room of a restaurant, a concert hall, an office building, a school. Anywhere but here. Anywhere that didn't hurt as much.

The waiting, the waiting, the waiting—it was part of the requirement, as if all the judge-switching and delayed agreed order-writing would wear you down to the point where you just gave up, gave in, and went home. And when you got home, you waited for the bill to arrive.

The courtrooms where divorce cases were heard were as crowded as those in domestic violence court, although the dance here was more subversive, less raw. Here the responses were practiced and the deceit strategic, all the posturing to prove a point. In domestic violence court, no one seemed to have a plan other than to live through the day.

At first, the visits to divorce court were several times a month, then slowly lessened to an appearance every six weeks or so. Sole custody was decided in my favor, a strictly limited visitation that included no overnights for the first three years after he left, child support and alimony, court-ordered therapy for the children, and court-ordered psychiatric reports, then a tango of appearances starring his objections to the results of the psychiatrist's recommendations. Then the objections to increased child support, though after three years, his salary had almost doubled since the divorce agreement. Then the changes in visitation. Then delays and more delays and more monthly bills in play-money amounts.

And though I mostly prevailed for myself and my children, the process was exhausting and demeaning. And so expensive. There was never a true sense of victory or calm, because I knew almost as soon as I left that there would be an appeal or an argument, or he would fight a decision. I never once walked into the building or left it feeling anything but depressed.

It had all been such a horrible education. I didn't know July 26, 1995, when he called to say he was filing for divorce in two days, that this would evolve into such a long, arduous emotional and financial burden. I thought just being divorced was punishment enough. I thought the worst thing about it would be telling the world your marriage had failed and the father's name would be absent from your children's class directories.

On April 24, 1996, the afternoon before we were set to appear in divorce court at 2 P.M. for the "Judgment for Final Dissolution of Marriage," he called off the divorce. My sister told me the news. He had initiated a frenzy of phone calls to my attorney and his assistant the day before the divorce, saying he would not agree to the language of a permanent injunction for myself and the boys against him should there ever be physical violence or harassment. He was barred from "beating, striking, threatening, harassing, or interfering" with me, while he was prohibited from "physically disciplining or harming the children." To make him agree to the language of the injunction, I was barred from the same.

"The divorce is off; he will not agree," my attorney's assistant told me the evening before our assigned day in court with the judge, the one we had waited for for nine months.

"Let him hit her and the boys just once," his attorney said to David's assistant. "Then she can go get her order of protection."

The next morning my husband—we were still married then—called just after 10 A.M. to tell me that he would not go to the 2 P.M. appointment with the judge for the final settlement. "I never loved you," he told me.

My reaction took him off guard. He expected me to cry, he expected me to be hurt. I was, but I didn't show it.

"If you don't go today at two, then we are still married. You don't love me, you don't want to be married to me, just go and get it over with. Just show up." He told me again that he never loved me and that being married to me was the worst thing he ever did. I hung up the phone shaking. I felt then as I did the moments after a strike, when he was agitated and I would listen to his ranting and try to calm him.

I was tired of the game, but I was still playing. *This is the last time I will have to convince him of something,* I thought.

My attorney told me to come to his office, and we would proceed to court but not expect him to show up. When we arrived, he
was already there. I tried not to look at him, for the man who was
my husband seemed so foreign to me that it scared me. He was
laughing, smiling to himself. His hair was long. He was wearing
leather boots with heels. He looked as if someone else were dressing him, as if he were in a costume—his Divorce Day costume.

"Don't look at him," Madeleine warned me. "He's trying to
annoy you."

We sat in a judge's small chambers, my attorney, my mother, my
sister Madeleine, my brother Paul, and me. He sat on a chair tap-
ping his foot incessantly and hitting his right fist on his knee
rhythmically. Hand jive.

I thought the earth would swallow me whole when the words
met the air that we were declared divorced—these were words I
feared, words that meant I had failed, I had chosen wrong, I had
agreed to have my children grow up without a father. I had never
wanted it to end like this. I had loved this man, deeply loved this
man, and I had tried. I only wanted him to be the man he said he
was. I wanted him to be the man who meant the words he wrote
in all those cards, on all those flowers, long since dead.

Still, I was bursting with such contempt and shame for what he
had done, what I had done, and what we had done together to
destroy this family, this collection of lives dependent on our
promise to each other, now broken. I was angry at myself for gripping this lopsided dream so tightly that I could not see what was
really true. I was angry and shattered. My boys were now only
seven, five, and two. Colin was still in diapers; Brendan was in
preschool where everyone's mommy and daddy came to the
Christmas plays and sat together holding hands. Weldon was in
second grade, and he had already known more hurt than many of
my friends who had lived thirty more years.

"How old were you when your father died?" Weldon asked me
once in the car just after the divorce.

"Thirty," I replied, not thinking or trying to decipher the point of his question.

"I was six," he said dryly as he looked out the window.

It took me several seconds to be able to speak at all. And then I didn't have any idea what to say.

April 25, 1996. Nine months after he hit me for the last time, Judge Jordan Kaplan declared our marriage over. In a few sentences, twelve years of my life were erased. The judge looked across his desk at me, at him, his bifocals lowered on the bridge of his nose and pronounced us divorced, our marriage dissolved. It was over. As petitioner, my husband filed for divorce on grounds of irreconcilable differences. As the respondent, I countersued on grounds of physical abuse. I wanted that in the record permanently.

The words served as a guillotine to me, cutting me off forever from this blind dream I groped for, this dream of a family, a mom and a dad and three little boys, living happily ever after. From now on, I could no longer pretend. I was divorced. The dream was dead.

We all sat in Judge Kaplan's chambers, a room small, private, and clinical, unlike the courtroom with the public parade of pain and anguish. My mother looked on, the hurt on her face visible, and my brother looked sympathetic. My sister held my arms. He was laughing, congratulating his attorney, and walking away. As if he was proclaiming victory. I was waiting for his hand to shoot into the air in a fist.

"I am so proud of divorcing you," he told me later. "It is the best thing I ever did."

I was told by different people I knew that I would feel tremendous relief after the divorce was final, that it would be over, there would be no more conflict. I didn't feel that way at all. I felt more hurt, because now it was real. It was more affirmation that it had all happened. Yes, he had battered his wife. Yes, he had said all those things, done all those things, filed all those motions, written all those vicious letters. It was no longer a dispute that could be contained or hidden.

I was a battered wife. Now I am no wife at all.

It was intellectual consolation, I guess, that the judge gave me 100 percent of the house and sole custody of the children. The judge ordered my ex-husband would have limited visitation, no overnights for at least one year, though visits were not supervised. But I guess the people who told me I would feel a peace were not familiar with the profile of someone like my former husband. The abuse would continue.

"I'm going to take the children away from you," he would scream into the phone after the divorce. "I can always petition to have custody," he said. "You're psycho!" he would shout to me after visitations, as I waited at the front door while he stood by his car and my little boys tumbled to get out and run to the front steps.

"I'm going to fight your mother for you!" he would tell them. And then when he canceled his visits, sometimes after the time he was scheduled to appear, he would tell the boys later that I wouldn't let them come, that I was stopping him from seeing them.

Then he refused to pay the dental bills, the bills for emergency room visits—Brendan's stitches in his knee, Colin's stitches in his nose—and it was more fighting, more shouting matches that ended in names. "Pay for it all with your inheritance," he said.

So there were calls to the lawyers and the children's lawyer and the children's therapist; meetings and more meetings and more trips to court to prevent him from threatening me and calling names, to prevent him from coming into the house, to prevent him from bringing other people with him to my door, to answer his accusations, to counter his motions, to collect increased child support. And each maneuver cost more money than I had, spent more energy than I could give, and took more time than I could afford. But I fought relentlessly, knowing I had to keep my children safe and to keep him from manipulating every situation. And so it wasn't over. It isn't over.

Living within reach of a person who has abused you physically and continues to abuse you verbally feels just as it appears in all those scary B movies. There is usually a scene with a frightened young woman home alone—at night, usually when it's raining—and a killer on the loose. She locks the doors and the windows, and she sits on the couch, panting, hoping to feel safe, keeping her panic at bay. Is she safe yet? And then you see a hand at the window, a face at the door, and she screams. . . .

I spent many years feeling that insistent fear. During periods of time when he would not call or cause a conflict, I could not relish the peace; I could only act like the young girl in the movies, locking all the doors and windows, knowing he was outside trying to get in. I could only be vigilant and apprehensive, waiting for his intrusion, frightening as a hand at the door, the crash of the glass at the window. And it would always happen.

There would be an incident on a visitation, then a forceful denial, then an angry letter and a series of brutish calls. Sometimes calls from lawyers, sometimes legal action. Always costing money I didn't have. Money robbed from the future to pay for the past.

For the first year, just the sight of a letter with my attorney's firm's return address was enough to scare me. What is he doing to me now? What awful accusation must I respond to? What aggression requires my time and money and emotional energy? I no longer could open the letters immediately but had to wait until I was calm, the children were asleep, and I could brace myself for the copy of a letter he wrote or a copy of a motion he made.

Sometimes a letter from the attorney would sit unopened on the kitchen counter for two or three days. I didn't want to fight anymore. I wanted it all to stop. I wanted him to go away. For God's sake, I was even afraid of the mail.

There were the stream of letters referring to me not by name, but "my ex-wife," as if I were his possession, as if he controlled me.

"No, not today," I would say to myself. "I'm not opening it today."

Eventually I would open it, but it would take a few days. I would have to lie down on the living-room couch when the kids were asleep and read it there, breathing deeply, posturing myself so the aggression and the hatred he felt for me—translated into a court action and a lawyer's letter—would not sting as sharp.

There was the July 2, 1996, letter he wrote to the children's attorney and copied to me, one year after he left the house, following an incident when the boys said he threatened to throw them off a bridge. He later said he was telling them what he would do to save them if they fell off a bridge. "I just want you to die," he told Weldon when he was eight, and he admitted it to the children's attorney. He said he was sorry. He always had explanations. He always wrote letters.

"Just like Weldon," he wrote, "my ex-wife is attempting to fabricate facts that show me to be an unfit father. . . . My ex-wife is attempting to sabotage my relationship with the boys by insinuating destructive and false images of their father. . . . I understand that my ex-wife has difficulty dealing with my having found a loving relationship, but I will not allow her to use her anger as an excuse to attack me and the boys. She must learn to control her anger and stop thwarting my relationship with them. . . . My ex-wife's comments . . . expose her as someone who is more interested in attempting to impede my life than someone who cares about the welfare of the boys. She needs to find a constructive outlet for her life. Her anger toward me is destructive and unhealthy to the boys."

It was a race always to keep up with him—I could never stay ahead—to try to counter his aggression. When I would relax, he would surprise me with a threat, such as the time in 1996 before I took the boys to Michigan for a week, when he called to tell me he was getting a court order to say I could not take the boys out of state.

It was absurd, my attorney said; I have sole custody, he has no grounds, but it scared me nonetheless. *To be safe, I just won't answer the door or the phone. That way I can't be served with anything.* Once again, he made me afraid. The abuse had not stopped even though the man who abused me was out of the house. I was still living in fear.

"Look at it this way, you're no longer afraid every day of your life," my friend Vicki told me.

There was the time in 1995 he brought the police to the door to make sure I cooperated with visitation, a show of force, another form of abuse. I had not denied visitation; it was just to show me he could do that to me. What followed was another trip to court to have a court order saying that he could not involve the police in anticipation of a problem and that having my little boys terrified by their father bringing police to the house was not in their best interest. Little Brendan, four, had sat on the steps in tears. And later he filed a criminal action against me because I would not give Colin (who was one) to him because he was ranting at the door and pounding on the windows to get in, enraged, even though the court order required him to stay in the car at the curb.

"I know what you are like when you act this way, and I will not hand over my baby to you," I told him. An Oak Park police officer had told me I should do that if I feared his behavior, that it was better to explain it to a judge later than risk the children being hurt. "Trust your instincts," the police officer told me. My ex-husband later dropped the charge.

Each time in the courtroom, each time having a public battle, I wished I was someone else, that I didn't have this life, that I no longer had to contend with someone shamelessly unpredictable. I wished I did not have to forever deal with this man who, because he could no longer abuse me physically, would do what he could to hurt me legally, financially, emotionally.

I would look around at the faces of the other women and think how I never imagined I would be in this room. *I never thought this would happen to me. I bet none of you thought it would happen to you. But we are here. Just as in domestic violence court. Just as in the group sessions at Sarah's Inn. I never thought I would be in any of these places. Funny how things turn out.*

One morning in 1995, as I was waiting in court seated on a bench on the right, waiting for his name to be called from the docket (since he was listed as petitioner, it was always his name), I sat with Bob, my attorney, who was trying to distract me.

Standing before the judge was a man wearing what looked like a European suit, double-breasted and pale gray. He wore those soft leather loafers you see on men in gangster movies. His shirt was open; he wore no tie. He had salt-and-pepper hair, long for a man in his forties, past his ears, resting on the top of his jacket.

I strained to hear what he was telling the judge.

"I need an emergency order freezing our assets," he pleaded to the judge.

The judge asked him to explain.

"She already took $18,000 in cash from one account, the 1987 Porsche, and our daughter. I haven't seen her for three days."

Bob leaned over to me and whispered in a deadpan, "I bet she's not coming back."

I smiled. It shouldn't have seemed funny, but it did. I could look at this case, this broken couple, and smile because finally it wasn't me up there, naked with my hurt. She got the Porsche, the cash, and her child. She had enough. She wasn't coming back. I knew he was in pain, that they had their own story of betrayal and hurt, but it still seemed morbidly funny. I pictured his wife and her daughter laughing, like Thelma and Louise, riding in the Porsche, free, away from the courtroom forever.

I knew she wasn't coming back. Who would?

I'm quite sure it was the only time in that building I ever felt anything close to good.

Card received on my birthday, June 5, 1989

You are the joy of my life. I love you more and you mean more to me than all God has given me. Little Man, our son, an expression of our love, will be the constant beacon of where this love will take us—in God's hand.

13

A Safe Place

"Can I have my birthday party at Sarah's Inn?" Brendan asked one day in July, planning far in advance his fifth birthday party in January. His question was so remarkably innocent, as if the domestic violence services agency was McDonald's or Chuck E. Cheese. "I love it there," he said.

I kissed the top of his head.

I had been taking the boys to Sarah's Inn once a week since the Monday in July after their father left our home. I did not want to let anything that had happened to us become suffocated in explanations; my children needed to know that the truth was not too terrible to say out loud. They needed to know that whatever the truth was, it should not be buried, suppressed, denied. I knew they needed help sorting through the debris this volcano had left, and I knew exactly where to go.

I tried to think what it was like for them: In one day that summer, their father was gone, their mother couldn't stop crying, and the whole world was different. All the rushing and slamming of doors, all the secret talks, the hiding, and past explanations they knew didn't ring true could now be explained. They needed to be loved and comforted, and they needed to say out loud that they were hurt, afraid, and mad. And they needed to say it to someone who wasn't me—or him—someone who knew exactly what to say so there would be no scars. They needed to speak out loud everything and anything in their hearts to someone who wouldn't shush them quiet and tell them it wasn't really true.

Brendan and Weldon were in a children's group with Dorothy, the children's program coordinator, whom they learned to love and respect. In their one-and-a-half-hour sessions, they drew pictures, had group "talks," and played games with other children who were suffering and healing and who could share their same feelings. They learned right away their lives need have no shame.

A year later representatives from Sarah's Inn came to Willard School, where Weldon was in second grade, for a school assembly about abuse and safety. With tears in her eyes, Weldon's teacher later told me that Weldon had raised his hand and stood up, said his name, and asked them to please say "hello" to Dorothy for him because she was his friend.

His teacher told me she was so proud of him. I was proud because he had accepted the truth and showed he was not ashamed.

It was a place where they learned to feel safe about telling; it was a glorious place where they learned their feelings had merit and that abuse is not something to hide. Weldon went another afternoon after school during the week to talk to a therapist one-on-one for an hour. Brendan was too young, they said. Colin was not yet two. At Christmas, this woman gave Weldon a blue polished stone, and she told him to hold it when he felt afraid. He made her a card.

After their last session, I had gone to pick him up in her office, after climbing the two flights of stairs, carrying Colin and holding Brendan's hand. I had canceled a play date for Weldon because of his appointment here. And I was tired, feeling overwhelmed and sad that my boys didn't just play at friends' houses after school, that their lives were so complicated they came to therapy at a domestic violence services agency.

The therapist opened her door and came out with Weldon, and they were laughing. His face was bright and he was smiling, and I felt so relieved I started to cry. She came over to me and said, "He's such a great kid." Then she turned to him and brushed his hair with her hand and said, "Weldon, you're very cool."

"Is he going to be okay?" I blurted out, as if she was a medical doctor, diagnosing him for some affliction, looking into her crystal ball as if she knew the answer.

"Sure, he's great," she said and put her arm around me. "He'll be fine."

A few more tears came out, and I laughed nervously, feeling such unfathomable relief. I didn't feel so tired anymore; I felt truly elated. This was a moment of pure joy for me. I drove the boys to get ice-cream sundaes to celebrate. They thought it exceptionally odd because it was almost dinnertime, but I didn't want to be sensible. I wanted to celebrate. Whenever I think about Sarah's Inn and the enormously positive effect it had on my family and on me, I think of that therapist and the gift she offered me that moment, and I am grateful.

It is a place where I learned I could relax and have the boys tell about the anger and the sorrow they felt. It was a place where I felt the same.

At first the separate weekly meetings the boys and I attended were open meetings on Monday, and anyone could come into the group. One of the first weeks I attended, a woman who had been there for months asked me why I was wearing my wedding ring. I said I didn't know and started to cry.

I didn't know when I was supposed to take it off. If we're not divorced, we're still married, right? I've been wearing this ring since 1985. I have never taken it off. Should I now? Is that what you do? Please guide me.

She told me to try taking it off sometime and see if I wouldn't feel better.

It was another vivid moment among many at Sarah's Inn, where I started to heal, a piece at a time, an inch of flesh at a time, each day new cells filling with hope and a future that was not tainted by new hurt. Beginning in September, the boys and I attended weekly closed meetings—meetings with the same people each week. In the children's group, the boys were with the same eight or so children, many their ages. In the women's group, the same ten or twelve women showed up dutifully.

If one woman missed a week, we all worried. So if we knew there would be a problem or conflict ahead of time and we had to miss, we called the women's coordinator to explain the absence in advance so no one in the group would be concerned. We made sure each other was all right.

We listened to each other and cried, trusting each other with our secrets, developing friendships, as if this was as commonplace as a book club or a volunteer group. We laughed. We did therapeutic, guided exercises and set goals. Some women lived at Sarah's Inn, in temporary housing with their children. Some of us lived in our own homes and apartments. Some of us had jobs and brought our children in for the 6:30 meetings with bags of carryout food. We occasionally spoke on the phone with each other. Once another client and her two daughters came to our house for dinner.

The months that I went there, I lived this oddly dichotomous life, where I worked and shuttled the boys to swimming and school, basketball, language class, and after-school sports. Living the American dream with a house in the suburbs and children who were clean and well-fed, I would appear to any objective observer as blessed as every other modern mother with a carpool full of small children and a list of errands that needed to be done.

But once a week I drove to Sarah's Inn, where I saw no one I had ever known before. It seemed to be a place in such contrast with the rest of my life, but a place where I could really be who I was. At first I felt relief that I could say these things out loud and no one was shocked. Then I felt depressed that I was labeled a type, a photograph in a psychology book with the caption, "Battered Wife." But when I started to learn about the other women there and absorb their kindness and connect to their wisdom, I learned we could not all be a type, we could not all fit in a chapter.

There is no one type.

Each of us was different, in age, race, appearance, experience, careers, and lifestyles. But all of us were worthy of being loved; none of us deserved any of this, asked for it, wanted it, searched for it. What we had in common was our desire to heal.

If I would run into any of the women from Sarah's Inn outside of the group sessions, we would embrace each other warmly. Sometimes it was at the grocery store, the park, the local YMCA. Once at a stoplight, I saw a woman from Sarah's Inn in her car next to mine, and we honked and waved at each other. *See? We're out in the world and we're fine!* I wanted to shout.

One evening in a group session, a woman was telling a story about her ex-husband who had hurt her with knives and who had been cruel to her in ways we all could imagine. But it was the words she used to explain the things he said that struck me most. When she was finished, I said, "It seems like we married the same man."

She smiled and said, "I don't know about you, Honey, but mine was black." We were all so different, so much the same.

Each week, we kept each other informed on our progress, what we were feeling, what had happened in court, on visitations, with our children. We shared advice on coping in the courtroom. One woman said she couldn't even watch a wedding—even ceremonies in movies or sitcoms on television—without feeling the anger and frustrations she felt because her own marriage ended.

In one meeting, the coordinator handed us a typed list of warning signs to watch in partners who may become abusive. There were about fifteen attributes listed, from "controls finances" to "calls names." I'll never forget the shock I felt reading that simple, typed sheet. Every item listed—except the one about drug and alcohol use—was true for me. It was as if abusers followed a textbook, chapter by chapter, and they all did the same things, committed the same acts, the same betrayals.

One woman was remarried and wrestling with issues of trust and raising her son away from his father. Another survivor was dating a man whom she feared was controlling. Another woman, barely in her twenties, was being stalked by her former boyfriend, a man she had been dating since she was thirteen. He was the only man she had ever loved.

Another woman in the group cried as she told the story of her husband, who would come home after a night of drinking and terrorize her, shouting, calling her names, chasing after her. Another woman talked about her boyfriend, who would get high on cocaine or crack and then inevitably bang on her door late at night, angry, accusing. And then he would hurt her once she gave up and let him in.

Many of the women nodded. It was worse with alcohol. It was worse with drugs. They talked about being afraid if their husbands drank too much at parties. If they were late coming home from work, it would only mean that they had been drinking. The cycle was predictable. If drugs or alcohol were present, they would be abused.

The other women talked about how they tried to keep their partners sober, how they tried to keep them straight. I never had those fears—my husband was hyper-healthy and worked out furiously, an hour or more each day. He avoided using even over-the-counter drugs, and he needed to be coaxed into taking cough medicine if he was sick. In twelve years, I never saw him drunk. I guess I was grateful that the violence in our home was not adhered to the relentless cycle of addiction. But the abuse still happened, even without it. There was one less thing to blame it on; there really was no excuse.

Sometimes the feelings I articulated in the group sessions would make me angry all over again, and I would be seething at him when he phoned to talk to the boys, once a week or less. It was hard to reveal the things he had done and then speak to him on the phone calmly, as if nothing had happened. I was so angry I wanted the world to know what he had done to me. I was so angry I wanted him to be punished. The anger was powerful; it had taken nine years to gain momentum. *How can what he has done be dismissed?*

Then sometimes I wanted to ignore the past, never return to

Sarah's Inn and the honesty it forced. Sometimes I wanted to hide and act as if I was like every other mother with a station wagon full of children. Sometimes I didn't want to talk about how terrible I felt and tell somebody else the truly demeaning and horrific acts he had done to me. I could think of a hundred better ways to spend a Wednesday evening.

But then I would know that the boys looked forward to going, and they would talk about the baseball hats they would decorate and how Dorothy was waiting for them. And we would go. I never missed a session, nor did they. I hired a sitter for Colin and went.

And every time I walked up the stairs to the session room, I was always glad I had gone.

Their father, of course, did not endorse this practice. He was adamantly against the boys going to the sessions. And though I had sole custody and I could take the boys where I felt I needed to take them, his attorney tried to stop me. His attorney told Bob that it was just baby-sitting for me and that the boys were being told to hate their father. Bob responded that it was not baby-sitting because Colin could not go, and I needed to hire a baby-sitter at our house so the boys and I could attend.

My husband's attorney called Sarah's Inn and began shouting on the phone and asking questions, the counselor told me in a later session. They were not allowed to reveal names of any clients, so they offered her no information about us and would not confirm our attendance. She didn't scare them, they said. Nor did he. They would be our advocate.

At a court appearance in late 1995, the judge ordered that Weldon and Brendan receive counseling from a private, court-appointed children's therapist and discontinue their counseling at Sarah's Inn. My husband's lawyer argued that the children were alienated from their father because of what they were told at Sarah's Inn. My lawyer argued that was not the case and that the services at Sarah's Inn were free of charge and quite helpful to children of abusers in adjusting to the aftermath of abuse.

The judge ordered that the cost of the children's therapist be split between my husband and me after his insurance paid half, with my husband paying the bulk of the remaining costs. Though I was against it (mostly because I could not handle another burden of expense), this therapist became a godsend, helping my boys immensely. In the months and years he saw Weldon and Brendan, he sorted through the maze of their feelings, expertly and sensitively, in ways I didn't know how to do. He offered me critical advice and suggestions on guiding them through their anger and managed to develop a sincere, trusting relationship with them, offering them another safe haven to express themselves. A kind and compassionate man, they grew quite fond of him and still want to give him gifts on holidays. Sometimes Brendan thanked God for him in our prayers before dinner. Colin begged to go talk to him too, though he was too young.

"I want to have a job like him when I grow up," Brendan said to me once, unprompted, as I was making dinner. "You sit in a big chair in a nice house, smile, and listen and say, 'Uh, huh, yes, uh, huh, yes.'" He paused. "Then you tell them what to do, and everyone likes you."

Even though it was their father's suggestion for the boys to get help from this private counselor, and the outcome appeared highly successful, their father refused to pay what he owed in substantial fees and argued that his insurance company paid his portion and that the remainder was up to me. It was just one more fight, one more conflict. So I paid monthly installments, knowing that the best was done for the boys.

At Sarah's Inn, the best was done for them there too. The boys had completed six months of sessions before they were forced to stop. They attended the graduation of their private group, and Weldon has his Achievement Award certificate from the program taped to the inside of his closet. Brendan occasionally wears the white baseball cap they decorated on the last day of the session.

With the help of that safe place, I felt my sons and I were guided through the crisis. It was as if we all had been burned, but I had placed the skin under ice water so quickly there wasn't time for it to blister and redden too badly. We had burns, to be sure, and they hurt them and me. But the wounds had been tended to before they had a chance to fester.

For years, the boys openly talked about the abuse, at times to people they had just met and at school with their teachers. At his annual checkup with the doctor, Brendan would spontaneously explain about their father leaving our house and why. I asked each of their teachers, when the boys said something about their father or the past, to please never tell them to be quiet, but just to listen, hug them, and listen more.

What we really needed—what all abused women really need—was a safe place to learn to confront the truth.

Card received on July 28, 1993

Dearest Michele,

The picture reminds me of the pin I bought for you in Dallas. I loved to buy you clothes and accessories. It was a sign of my love for you that I could contribute to something that was such an important part of you—your clothes.

I know it is such a difficult time for you. You fight rejection continually for work that you know is beyond compare. Well, I can only say that I believe in you and I pray for you constantly. You will succeed. Your dreams will come true. Just stay attuned to the abilities God has given you. They will come to fruition.

I also know what a tremendous mother you are. The boys have all of their needs met, perhaps more than they should. I realize that you feel like an alien with all of these boys around the house. All I can say is that we love you and we won't lose sight of what you mean to us.

I love you.

14

Daddy Envy

The October evening after my first son, Weldon, was born in 1988, my husband called a close friend from the hospital room at Medical City in Dallas to tell the news. He cheerfully listed the baby's height and weight—eight pounds, two ounces, twenty-two-and-one-half inches—and offered a superficial, abbreviated version of his birth.

"We're going to have a whole tribe," he said triumphantly to his friend, I guess in his response to the question if we would ever do this again.

As I laid there on the hospital bed, exhausted, worried, and in more pain than I ever imagined, a catheter inserted and a doughnut of ice underneath me, I thought that was a powerfully optimistic statement. I had just been through twenty-two hours of labor, an intensely complicated birth, and Weldon was now— three weeks premature with a breathing difficulty—recuperating in neonatal intensive care.

But I also felt warmed by his exclamation. He was a father, a father as clueless and endearing as the ones in the black-and-white movies. He was a dad, a bumbling, sweet, Jimmy-Stewart kind of dad. I was charmed by the boyishness of his proclamation, and I felt relieved, as if all my fears during the pregnancy were lifted and the memory of his hitting me was annihilated in that one comment. He will be a good father. We will be a family—maybe someday a big family—and he will be the father I prayed he would be, proud and loving and engaged, participating, present. The chief of a tribe.

As the years unwrapped—some brittle, others smooth—and parenthood unfolded, it became apparent that the night in the hospital room was not a clear fix on the future. There was always a certain ambivalence mixed with impatience that characterized fatherhood at our house. He was rarely how I thought he would be. He was nothing like my father. He was nothing like his own.

By the time he was out of the house in 1995 and appeared at first to be slowly vaporizing from the children's lives, I developed a keen sense of Daddy Envy, a jealousy so blatantly green and exaggerated I could barely stand to go to the zoo on a Saturday to see fathers play with their sons. Christmas cards with a mom and a dad cuddling their brood proudly could do me in for a week, a month, a season.

The first pangs began shortly after he left, and I was consumed with the guilt and grief that not only had I ended a marriage, shotgunning a man who acted violently from my life, but I also had taken away my boys' father. For all the crimes he committed against me, there were the persistent idyllic notions of games of tackle football on the lawn and "monster" in the basement that the boys relished. I had nuked their chance for a father.

The notion that some divorced men have of ex-wives, I have learned, is that we are a seething, venomous lot hissing and spitting on the memories of the fathers of our children, forbidding the sons and daughters to love their fathers, performing rituals of erasure that keep them locked from their lives. While I insist on protecting my children and keeping them safe, I mourn, deeply mourn, their loss of a daily live-in father. They do not have what I had; they never will. They do not have a father who loves their mother fiercely. And I mourn that I do not have a husband who places me and my children above everything else.

They do not come home from school each day knowing Dad will walk through the door with stories and salutations, a looming presence gregarious and loving, giving them gifts of moments they crave, memories they will cling to. They don't see their father embrace their mother and know what that kind of security means. Love between a husband and wife does not last forever. That love lasts awhile. And love for a child is when it's convenient.

"Dodgeball always bothered me," my friend Ellen said, recalling my ex-husband's ritual game in the backyard on Linden Avenue when the boys darted back and forth across the small lawn. "It was his hitting them with the ball and then telling them they couldn't cry like a baby that got me," she said.

It got me too. I remember the same curl in my stomach during those games. I told him to play softer, and he told me the boys would be sissies if it was up to me. So I swallowed my instincts.

Driving down Linden Avenue in Oak Park in mid-July, only a few weeks after he left our house, I saw a father riding his bike behind his daughter, a ponytailed girl of perhaps five or six riding her own training-wheeled bike with bright pink plastic ribbons dancing from the handlebars like kite streamers in the wind. He was riding behind her, and she was ahead of him, laughing. The sight made me sad, it made me angry, it made me ache. Disappointment for myself, an adult, is heartbreak enough, but feeling as if the choice I had made will forever disappoint my children is paralyzing. I chose this man not only to be my husband. I chose him as their father. Three times, I made the choice.

Fathers in parades, fathers with children on their shoulders, fathers holding toddlers' hands, fathers sitting in restaurants laughing with their children, fathers cheering at T-ball games, fathers crossing a street pushing a stroller. I don't know what hurt more to watch, fathers taking their responsibility alone or fathers and mothers together, holding small hands between them, talking, laughing, like a picture in a magazine.

I will always be doing this alone. They will never have both of us at once. And while I can give them everything from me, I cannot give them him.

From the research and therapy I have completed, I have come to understand that it is a given that children want both parents; they want them to love them unconditionally, and they want them to love each other. For many it is a wish automatically granted. But for my sons, it was an impossible wish. The thought of not being able to facilitate and fulfill their primal desire nearly destroyed me.

In all the sessions with all the therapists, I learned this driving wish for an intact family is innate and ruthless, as if a family with one parent is so lopsided it can never be enough. I only once heard someone refer to my family as "children of a broken home," a phrase that made me cringe.

Their father hit me. I had to make him leave. He chose not to come back, not to try to get better. But I stayed, and I will always be here. I am not broken. My children are not broken.

What the courts and the books on divorce suggest is to minimize conflict for the sake of the children—that wise old saying—and learn to co-parent. Co-parent, as if you are co-piloting an airplane safely to a landing. It's a good image, a respectable goal, but so far it has been impossible for me.

In my case, there was a permanent injunction against further physical or verbal abuse. And now I could call him if I needed him to pick up the boys from basketball because I was late coming home from work? The notion was ridiculous.

It was naive to imagine that a man who for a dozen years could not be cooperative would suddenly, magically, become an ideal co-parent. In three years there were perhaps four conversations that were not laced with extreme bitterness, where he didn't accuse or I didn't remind him of his inconsistencies. He hung up on me in most every conversation, ones he initiated. It was nearly impossible for me not to be angry with all he had done and continued to do. I know I was bitter. Daddy Envy tainted every view.

Because of me, my boys do not have a father in their lives every day. I picked him. Why didn't it work as I planned? Why couldn't I see before our wedding day that this is where it would end? How can I stop feeling this guilt?

I knew intellectually it was not my fault. But I never would have chosen this for them. All I wanted in life was for my children to grow up happy with two parents who loved each other and loved them equally. I could adjust to my loss. It is much harder adjusting to theirs.

"Your boys absolutely don't experience him the way you do," my therapist told me. "He abused you. You are separate. Even the most horrific parents are loved loyally by their children," she said.

My boys do love him. Regardless of all he has done to me, affecting all of us, he is their father. He is handsome and fun and takes them to T.G.I. Friday's and Planet Hollywood for dinner. He buys them Nintendo games and Star Wars figures. In spite of the past, in spite of the present, in spite of it all, the boys want to be loved by him. They want him to want them. They want a father.

Regardless of the love I give them, it is not enough. They want their father too. And no matter what I give them, I cannot give them that. It is a haunting, insatiable burn knowing that all I give them is not all that they need.

They will never have the regular reassurance of a father's hands, feeling, knowing how they are different from mine. A mother's hands are busy, kinetic; smoothing hair, straightening shirts, tucking in, rubbing muscles, massaging backs. My hands are purposeful and soft, carrying them to the car or gently washing the remnants of breakfast off small round cheeks. My hands are only for them when they are sick, wiping, stroking, taking temperatures, calming down. No matter what I am to them, I am not like them. They just are different from me. My thoughts, my joys, my life, my hands. Different from a boy's, different from a man's. Different from a father's.

A father's hands can be stronger, bigger, sometimes motionless, still reminders of a solid, lasting love. I remember my own father's hands and how they would sit on my shoulders if we were posing for a photograph, and how they felt on my back as he guided me on my first two-wheeler bike. They were large and warm, the strength of them understood, a silent reassurance. I remember as an adult how a hug from my father was different than my mother's, more forceful, filled with a different, bolder affection.

My mother's hugs were soft and tender, more often, with many more meanings. And I needed them both to feel balanced, to feel loved and accepted and whole.

A father's hands are also the athletic hands, the hands throwing, catching, guiding, lifting. The hands pulling sleds, pushing rafts, pulling ropes, guiding bikes, making knots, hammering, fixing. Their father's hands are long and lean, powerful, skilled. He has athletic hands, graceful and firm, capable. The hands around a baseball bat, the hands in a catcher's glove. The strong, hard hands in a boxing glove, their movements calculated, pointed. The hands that could teach them to play anything.

I go to the boys' games—soccer, baseball, basketball, floor hockey, touch football—and I cheer. Sometimes I am impatient, chasing Colin around fields, courts, and playgrounds, waiting for the next play, the next inning, the next time up, looking at my watch, *when will it be over?* A lot of the times, I am wishing I wasn't the only one there. And if he is there, I wish he was someone who loved me too. I see how my sons react to the fathers who are their coaches, and sometimes they say how much they like the men and how their dad would never be a coach. And sometimes, true, they say they are glad they don't have a father like the coach who yells too much or makes them feel ashamed if they make a mistake. And sometimes they ask me why I didn't marry this coach or that father there. *Him? Why don't you marry him now?*

"Are we getting a new dad for Christmas?" they ask every year.

My children will never know a daily difference, comparing a father's hands to a mother's touch. They will not run from room to room in our house, from my arms into the arms of their father. There is only a stiff, anger-swallowed transfer when he stands in the driveway by his black Toyota Land Cruiser and I stand by the front door.

Have a good time. Call me.

I must trust that my boys will decide for themselves how they will define their father and how they will process the dramatic complications forced into their lives. While my anger for what he has done to me has subsided, perhaps even diminished, my disappointment for them is infinitely harder to overcome. I cannot give them a father, and I had to take the one they had away. I can forgive myself sometimes, but can they forgive me?

That question leads them to more questions only I am there to answer.

"Why didn't you marry Uncle Paul?" Weldon asked me once, angrily, after we spent a few days with my brother and his family in Michigan. "He's a nice man and he wouldn't hurt his wife. He's an awesome dad."

Never mind explaining to an eight-year-old that it is illegal and unwise to marry your own brother, I understood what he meant. How could I be so unfair? How could I have chosen so poorly, knowing all that was at risk?

"How long did you date Dad before you married him?" Weldon asked me another day.

I explained it was three years, and he paused.

"Date the next guy for ten."

A few weeks before my husband left, we spent a June Sunday at the public beach in Evanston, a sanctuary where families with small children full of sand played on a clean, broad stretch of calm.

I had packed us all a lunch, and the requisite toys, towels, and diapers for Colin. I packed sunscreen, dry clothes, sheets, a blanket to park on, and hats for all the boys. I started packing right after 9:30 Mass at Saint Giles down the street and finished an hour later.

My husband went reluctantly. I hesitated to include him—mostly I went with friends and their children—because he worked most Saturdays and Sundays or he wanted to lie on the couch, watch TV, or read. I was going with the boys whatever he decided, I said. And he said he would come with us.

I drove as usual, because he was always too tired. And as he sat in the front passenger seat and slept, there was a keen sense that this was an unwilling traveler, a forced participant.

When we got to the beach, he plopped down on the sand. I worked around him, unpacking, organizing. The boys were running in different directions, crying for sunscreen, crying because they got sunscreen, begging to go in the water, begging not to go in the water. He just sat, uninvolved. A stranger.

A few yards from where we gathered on the blue-and-gold-plaid-sheet near the rust-flowered blanket—the Sears bedspread from my first apartment—was an older woman, fully dressed. She was pleasant looking with silver hair under a broad strawhat, a clear, smooth face, inviting and smiling. She was in her sixties, I guessed, and was sitting in a beach chair a few feet away from another family. She nodded hello. It wasn't obvious if she was with that family or if she was alone. She just seemed content to sit and watch us all.

Hours passed and he stayed on the blanket, detached. I chased the boys, played catch, built castles, and laid out lunch on the blanket. As we ate, he said a few stunted words, annoyed, bothered, filled with disdain. The boys were too loud; there was sand in his lunch. He didn't want what I packed him. It was hot, the sun bothersome. He engaged in a few more words at the meal, chomping his sandwich and sighing. I was unaware that the woman was watching us intently.

After another hour or two, it was time to leave. The boys had reached their limit of sun and sand, and I was packing up to go. He was still sitting, a transparent ghost. The dynamics of our family were public, though it ceased to humiliate me anymore. I would tell him how mad I was at his behavior later in the car. But now I would just pack up, get the boys together, and go. As I placed some of the toys in a red plastic laundry basket, I looked up to see the older woman looking right at me, right through me.

"Your boys will be fine," she said with such stern conviction it made me shiver.

I stopped for a moment, because her words were so sharp and

purposeful. The sincerity in her voice and the kindness in her eyes gave me pause.

"You will be fine. Your boys will always have you," she said.

Her comment was a gift. I felt, right there, as if I had been visited by an angel. *She sees, she understands.* It made me wonder if she could gather from the way he spoke to me, the way he did not speak to me, if she understood what I could not see, what I had closed my eyes to shut out.

Months later her words played over in my head, a calm chorus of encouragement. "Your boys will be fine," she assured me. "They have you."

Your boys will be fine. *Are you sure? Are you really sure?*

I see what my choices and blind optimism have done, and I regret above all else that what I can't give to my children is a father who is there for them every day, a man who loves their mother, a man who shows them how to be a good father and a good husband to their mother.

I am so heartily sorry that they don't enjoy a basic right of having a father whom they emulate and revere, a man who can show them how to be a good husband, who can show them how to love. I am sorry in the same way that I am sorry when they get hurt, fall down, hit their heads, scrape a knee, bruise an elbow, catch a cold. I know I didn't cause it, but I am sorry just the same. I just don't want them to suffer. I'm an adult and chose to love him, but they had no choice in choosing him as a father.

Forgive me. Forgive me.

My friend Jean told me recently that most every woman she knows has had her own close call with abuse, whether it was a boyfriend or a spouse who momentarily lost control. The question, she says, is not how can this happen so often, but how can it not?

I married a man I knew my whole life, a man from a similar background, a handsome, proud, athletic, religious man, a man from a good family, with an education, drive, ambition. In my parents' generation, it seems, this was all you could ask for. This would be the right equation. This should have worked. I inherited the same simple optimism. You presuppose a certain justice in the universe, and you believe—in every cell of your body—that the best will happen. And of course, you hope.

This is why so many women stay. This is why I stayed. You just hope.

My furious Daddy Envy period lasted at least a year, then it mellowed. I now only have it in fits and starts, mostly at holidays. In that initial time, I didn't like my friends' husbands playing with my children because it didn't make them feel better; it made them feel worse. They would come home and tell me how mad they were I didn't marry someone like Phil, Uncle Mike, Uncle Bill, or Uncle Ken.

Look what I don't have. Look what you've done to us, Mom.

If given a choice, no mother wants a child to grow up fatherless. When it does happen, you only work around it, hoping you can fill your children up, that you can compensate, love them enough, care enough, understand enough.

Once, maybe twice a year I get sick. Call-in sick, get-to-the-doctor, high-fever, antibiotics, don't-get-out-of-bed-for-a-day sick. It's usually because I am run-down, when months of five-hour sleep nights and running and rushing and working and ignoring what I need has taken its toll.

I can't totally stop, of course; three little boys can't suspend all their ricocheting needs, but I can cancel work and appointments. "Call in sick to your master," Brendan said once when I had the stomach flu. I can order Thai food for dinner and have it delivered. I can ask a friend to pick up the boys after school. I can do their homework with them from bed. I can skip a day of laundry. I can ask them to help make lunch.

But it's when I'm sick, feeling vulnerable and a little sorry for myself, that I cry. Not for myself so much, but because I wish that my boys could see that someone else in the family could take over, that it doesn't always have to be me or nobody. The original plan, the model that worked from the beginning, has two parents, so when one parent is filled up or burned out or just plain busy, the other picks up the slack. Ideally, both carry the family the whole way through.

I wish sometimes my boys could see that when I am out of the running—even if it is only for twenty-four hours—that their lives don't have to change. Because I think it's scary for them. When I get sick, Colin and Brendan always ask me if I am going to die. They tell me that's what scares them most.

"What will we do if you're dead, Mom?"

Yes, I did stay married to a man who acted violently. Yes, I did have three children with a man who hit me. And when I saw that it would never change, I made a choice for their father to go away so we could be safe, so my boys and I could live in a home without violence. So they would never again wake up and ask, "Did Daddy hit you?" So I would never again have to say yes.

Card received on Christmas, 1991

Dear Michele,

Next year in Jerusalem, as the saying goes, or Oak Park to be precise. I know many of your dreams will soon be fulfilled. I am so proud of the courageous stands you take in your column. Your success will be as normal as your God-given ability. You won't realize how significant it is until something or someone trips your insight.

Just think, in a few months we will be making plans for a new home. Chicago–Dallas–South Bend–Oak Park. I was never bold enough to dream we could make such a dramatic full circle the afternoon you sat on my lap in your office and told me the Dallas Times Herald *was recruiting you. We've been together for quite a ride. With our two sons in tow, we will be returning with more blessings than I could ever have asked. I commit my life to you this Christmas and always. May we always remember that the first love of our lives is each other. And with each other, we will find true joy.*

15

Sixty-Five Tears per Hour

Behind the wheel of my gray Volvo station wagon, I could let go of the volcanic grief inside me. There was something about the monotony, the banality of driving that made me feel safe enough to cry. Driving my car with the children strapped in their car seats, I could temporarily suspend attending to their needs. They were safe. It was then that my needs would come surging through.

The second week after my husband left the house following the emergency order of protection, the boys and I went to Lincoln Park Zoo with my friend Carol and her two daughters, Meg and Kathy. My boys were frenetic and anxious, insecure, uncertain. Dealing with three little boys under six was hard enough. Three angry, confused little boys was a whole other ball game.

But at least if I could pack us a lunch, if I could have a destination on this hot July day, be distracted and sheltered in the company of a kind, supportive friend, then I could control the hurricane I felt inside. *Three juice boxes, one Diet Coke. Three ham and cheese sandwiches. Weldon likes mustard. Brendan wants ketchup. Colin likes everything. Potato chips in three little plastic bags. An orange. An apple. Turkey on rye for me. We can buy cookies.*

No matter what I did, inside I was a maelstrom of raw hurt, confusion, and sorrow. When I was alone and I closed my eyes, the tears came of their own volition. I wanted a day off. I needed to do something other than feel bad.

We got near the zoo, and I started looking for a parking spot. I chose a small lot off LaSalle Street near the south entrance. I was driving and doing my best to concentrate on anything but the wicked jolts of hurt inside me. Carol and I were talking, and I was trying not to cry with every answer I gave her. When a driver in front of me needed to back up, I put the car in reverse without looking behind me, and I backed into another car. There was no damage and neither of us reported it, but I was so numb and so pained that I could not even feel the jar of hitting another car. I only heard the sound.

The children were upset. *Look what I've done now.*

After a few hours at the zoo, Carol said she would drive home. I got into the passenger seat and nearly collapsed. She drove to her house on Euclid Avenue, and I moved over to the driver's side and drove the three blocks to my house. I cried.

It happened every time I got behind the wheel. I could be in the car a few minutes feeling as if I could keep myself glued together long enough to reach my destination, and then it would start. Uncontrollably, involuntarily. I never knew I had so many tears inside.

I was crying for me, that I had been betrayed, that I lost a dream and I lost my husband. I was crying for my boys, that they had been dealt a legacy of violence. I was angry, my soul pitching between grief and a vicious anguish that grasped me at my very center. I was crying for a thousand reasons, and the reasons to cry kept multiplying.

I was crying because I wanted to be anyone but me. Because anyone else wouldn't need to cry this much.

When I was driving, I wasn't foolish enough to listen to any radio station but National Public Radio. Any other station might just play a song that would make me cry. I wasn't foolish enough to listen to any tapes that we enjoyed together. Anything but Wang Chung. The tape with "Start Me Up" by the Rolling Stones I had to throw away. It was too much him. I remembered us dancing. I remembered him holding me. I remembered feeling that he loved me. The music never reminded me of anything bad, only the good times, the in-betweens. With the violence, I also lost those years of in-betweens.

When I was pregnant with each of the boys, my husband would rub my swollen feet as we watched rented movies on the bedroom television. Every once in a while, he would make what we lovingly called "dirty carrot soup," a concoction that involved a whole chicken, carrots he didn't like to scrape clean, celery, vegetables, potatoes, and rice. It cooked on the stove all day in the large aliminum pot, and he doled out "tastes" when it was nearly finished, so proud of himself. It was a kind gesture, I thought, so I wouldn't have to make dinner. Sometimes in the kitchen when he was cutting and using every surface, he would sing to himself songs I'll never forget, and he would dance. The boys would laugh and say how funny he was.

I couldn't bear to hear those songs now.

On the radio I could listen to talk. Just talk. I could listen to strangers talking about accidents and traffic and politics and foreign eruptions. I could listen to book reviews and long news analyses and pretend I was comprehending, taking it in, as if there was any room left inside of me to absorb anything. If there was a news story involving domestic violence, I had to turn it off. It was too close. If there was a story about a murder, I couldn't bear it.

I could listen to the children's tapes, though. Raffi didn't make me cry. Tom Chapin was a relief, though references to Dad in a few songs made me feel worse.

I had stopped allowing Weldon to sit in the front seat when we drove somewhere. I told him it was because of the new safety law encouraging parents to have their children sit in the backseat. We didn't have air bags, but I didn't tell Weldon that. The real reason was that I wanted to cry without worrying that he saw me. He could sit in the back with Colin, while Brendan played in the third seat. It upset Weldon to see me cry, and I would cry a lot. Sometimes I just couldn't pretend I wasn't.

"Are you crying, Mom?" he would ask so often that I stopped lying and started to admit it.

"My heart is broken," I said more than once.

"Mommy's splitting," Brendan would say. And he was right.

"Right now? In half?" Colin would ask. "Can I see?"

I became afraid to drive and afraid to lie down. I knew that if I ever let go of the busy-ness of my life, the ache would devour me. I was afraid to lie in my bed, because when the boys were quiet and asleep in their beds, all that was left was me. And I felt like a wound, a gaping, oozing wound, sore and new. Without them to shield me, I had no one to hide me from myself. I was alone with the nakedness of my pain. I would lie in the center of the bed, and from belly-deep the tears would come.

Now that I am quiet, now that I am still, the tears must be heard, they must be felt.

So I did what I could not to lie down. I could never sit somewhere for long because then I could not avoid what was inside. If I was busy, if I was moving, the tears couldn't find a place to go, and I could contain them. I saw a television talk show once about a television newswoman who said she'd been so depressed and upset that she couldn't care for herself, her child, or even get out of bed. She just gave in.

I didn't want to lie down and be consumed. I wanted to keep moving so the pain would stay with somebody else. Working and caring for the boys afforded me a frenzy without room for tears. I couldn't afford to give in to the grief. Except when I drove. Except when I laid down at night.

At night I would sleep a few hours, then I would wake with a start and I would remember. I would remember the poisonous grief inside me, and I would want to retch or wash it away, drench it with the tears that had their own path. Tossing from my right to my left and back, I knew that I could not retreat from the torrents that stalked me. The tears were cleansing, and I felt if I could just cry enough, I could cry the hurt away.

Maybe I will cry forever.

I would concentrate on the tears and how they felt encompassing and strong. If I thought about crying, I didn't have to think about why. But then I would remember that I was alone with my three boys. I would remember that the man who was their father, the man who was my husband, was a man who had hurt me deliberately and who loathed me. And I would cry for what was, and I would cry for what wasn't. I would just cry.

It was the foreverness that would overwhelm me. I laid there in the dark, the streetlight shining through the white-painted paned window, the crisp cream cotton curtains wind-played, the boys in their rooms, innocent, asleep. I would tell myself that it will always be like this, that I will be consumed with the needs of my children all day and crying alone in my bed each night. I could see no other way. It seemed so endless. The tears kept coming. That summer. That fall. That winter. That next spring.

"You're so brave," my friend Jan said to me the day after he left. "You have just done the bravest thing for your family, taken away all your security." She meant it to be kind and reassuring.

Oh, my God. I've taken away their security. My boys are doomed.

When I drove, I felt the same rocking, relentless solicitation to release that I felt when I lay in bed. I could even begin a trip driving the children to school or on an errand with the resolve that I would not cry, and a few minutes into the trip, my eyes would be filled with tears. Involuntary hysteria. There had to be such a thing.

I was driving home one afternoon from the lawyer's office. Traffic westbound on the Eisenhower Expressway was molasses-slow, and I snailed along, elbows away from cars in the near lanes. On my right was a woman driving a red sports car; she was in her twenties or thirties with long blond hair, and she was sobbing. Her mouth was open, and her eyes were lobster-pink from the tears she had shed.

I see you! I wanted to shout. *I hear you! I feel what you feel.* I wanted to smile to her; I wanted to embrace her. I wanted her to know that traveling westbound at fifteen miles per hour on the Eisenhower Expressway, I was a crumbling batch of tears too. But she passed me. She never noticed me, crying behind my sunglasses.

The crying lasted for many months, almost a year. I cried so often when I was driving that I avoided driving long distances or late at night because I realized it was just not safe. I turned down invitations to dinner at restaurants more than a few miles away because I did not want to cry in the car. I stayed home and cried. I also learned that if I had a glass of wine, even at a party with friends, it would make me cry. So I wouldn't have one. The tears were worse if I did, because I felt too much, more than I could handle.

And when friends urged me to go out, to meet other men, to come to parties, to forget, I would sometimes surrender. Unless it was at the homes of my brothers and sisters or my friend Ellen, though, I always wished I hadn't taken someone else's solution for my own. I did not need to pretend I was okay. I just needed to cry.

I couldn't be superficial to the friends who couldn't comprehend what I felt. I felt my whole body needed to be washed cleaner, that if I could cry all the tears inside, the wound would start healing from underneath, growing new, stronger skin and tissue, not just a scar over the top. It would make me better, make me whole.

I didn't need to be in the arms of anyone else. I needed to be in my own arms. Crying.

I took baths to soothe myself. Alone at night in the tub I could recuperate, enjoy the silence. Look at a magazine. Stare at a catalog. Not worry. Just feel. Ellen gave me candles to light when I took a bath and impossibly luxurious bath oils. My sister Madeleine gave me a bath pillow and indulgent accessories such as loofah mitts and hair wraps and more lotions. Every night I could lie in a steaming tub, smell these wonderful smells, and cry. And I could be with myself and realize that crying was the right thing to do.

And so I surrendered to my habit, I surrendered to the feeling that this ocean of distress and sadness I carried with me daily would come out in spite of my directives to stay composed. And it would come out when I was in my room, when I was in the bath, and when I was driving.

In those months I didn't wear much mascara. I carried eyeliner pencil in my purse to reapply it. I carried with me blush, foundation, and powder to smooth over the stripes of tear stains on my cheeks. I wasn't proud I was so hurt, but I knew I had to be. So I allowed myself. And I cried me a river or two.

Then one ordinary day in June, almost one year after my ex-husband left, I drove to teach my class at Northwestern, up to Evanston and back—each way a one-hour trip—without crying. I was listening to a Madonna tape in the car. It was loud, teenager-loud, and I was singing along, shoulder dancing, feeling every word, every beat.

The windows were open, and I was driving fast. The children were at home. I was alone, and my God, I wasn't crying. I was singing. I didn't cry, not once.

I knew then I was getting better. I knew then I would be okay.

PART THREE

GETTING BETTER

Card received on Valentine's Day, 1991

M,

    It won't be long before we will be able to spend time together. I am grateful for your generosity and courage. Our lives are much more meaningful in relation to each other. We know how much we love and need each other. Thank you, Michele, for all your love. I love you so.

16

Gathering Strength

I wore my wedding ring to my twentieth high school reunion, Oak Park–River Forest High School, class of 1975. My husband and I had been classmates—with eleven hundred others—and because the reunion book was printed in advance, before the order of protection and before he filed for divorce, we were listed as married with three children.

But it was September 1995, two months since he had left and several weeks into the complicated divorce proceedings. I was embarrassed that I was no longer happily married to the boy who was voted a finalist in "King of Hearts." The track star, the model husband, the model man. The boy who could be voted as most likely to lead a charmed life if there was such a thing.

I could get the courage to get him out of the house, yes, but I wasn't yet able to tell the world about it or why. Certainly not at the high school reunion. People knew him there, or at least they thought they did. Would they think it was my fault? Wasn't it always the wife's fault? When anyone asked me where he was, I said he was busy. My good friends knew the truth and knew not to ask about it.

Halfway through the party at an Oak Brook hotel, I went to the ladies' room and put my wedding ring in my purse. I unzipped the inside pocket and put it there. And I kept it there, all night long.

Perhaps it was the sight of hundreds of familiar faces that made me see that I was someone well-liked and comfortable before him, before the abuse. It made me see—even if only for a few hours and for the first time since he left—that there would be more time in my life after him that was good and full and laughter-touched.

The clothes he bought for me were the next things that I needed to expunge to feel stronger, more independent, less tainted by him. I stopped wearing the blouses he bought me, the dresses, but the two pairs of pants that went with so many things were granted a reprieve to stay in my closet.

I dyed my hair a different shade—more golden brown instead of the daring red I tried our last Christmas together—and asked the stylist for a new style of cut: shorter, softer, with more layers. A divorcée cut. A no-longer-married-but-with-three-children cut. I continued taking long luxurious baths at night and wearing blueberry mud masks before I went to bed. I bought new bras—satiny, luxurious, lacy ones—and a short black leather jacket. I put a canopy over my bed. Long, sheer white panels cascaded from the sides, and I marveled at how feminine and majestic it looked.

God, he would have hated this.

I was gathering my strength, rebuilding who I was, and dreaming, every night dreaming about friends I knew in high school, friends I knew in college. Old boyfriends. Women I knew. People I liked, people who liked me. I wanted to be around people who knew me before I was this battered woman. This ex-wife. This victim.

I know now that I was trying to reclaim the woman—the girl—I was before I was a wife who was abused. I needed to return to the strength I knew was there all along and was only hiding under the twisted sense of loyalty I had to the man I loved and married, the man who hurt me. Before there was this brain game of power and surrender, there was a woman who could stand alone and succeed.

And I needed to know her again.

When I was twenty-three and lived in my first studio apartment alone on Wrightwood Avenue, in the building with the red-and-white striped awnings and gargoyles on the side, I had an emergency appendectomy. I remembered my slow recovery and how it hurt to walk more than a block, how exhausted I would feel if I needed to walk to the grocery store on Clark Street. It was the first surgery I'd had, and the way my body responded shocked me. I really couldn't do what I wanted to do. I had to slow down, rest, recover. For weeks I could not work full days at my job. I would get off the 151 bus and walk awkwardly from the bus stop to my office building on State and Adams. I felt frail and wounded. I felt old.

It was close to two months before I felt strong, solid, able to rely on myself, convinced of my sturdiness. Myself again.

Recovering from a violent relationship takes longer and is less obvious, but the feelings of weakness and slow recuperation are parallel. But the energy I had once used to camouflage the abuse was energy I was now using to heal and grow stronger. There were feelings I couldn't control: the crying, the grief, the physical pain of a broken heart. And I was so tired, tired from fighting.

"He is a violent man who will never change," said a therapist I went to see only days after my husband left in July 1995. Her downtown office was neat and chrome-accented, her tone straightforward and uncompromising.

"How do you know he will never change? You don't even know him." I was incredulous, defensive. I still thought he was coming back.

"I can say that definitively because of the duration of the abuse, because it escalated, because counseling did not help, and because he exhibits no remorse."

Do you mean he is not sorry because he tells the lawyers he was only trying to make me stop talking? Do you mean because he said I hit him? Do you mean to tell me he never loved me? Do you mean I am stupid?

I hated her. I hated what she said. *How in the hell does she know? How can he be a type? He loves me; he just needs help. He'll get better and he'll be back. You'll see. My life cannot be a total lie.* I left her office after writing her a check, and she handed me the business card of another therapist, just in case I might want to talk to her instead.

What did she mean he would never change?

I cried the entire way home, from the time I got in the car at the parking lot until I pulled into the garage at home, the half-empty two-car garage. I knew she was right.

He would *never* change.

You can't tell someone her truth, because she can't hear it. A personal truth must be realized at a high cost. The price of acknowledging my truth was hearing my four-year-old son say matter-of-factly, "Daddies make you purple."

It is the first Herculean task to accept the truth. The second is to act upon it. It is the next to rebuild yourself and gather the strength to move ahead, move forward, and stay committed to the truth. To see. To keep your eyes open. To battle the monsters tirelessly, to awe the gods with your strength, to outwit the plaguing deceptions as you try to get back to the truth.

At first I thought it would have been much easier to rebound from the abuse if I did not have my boys, the constant worry and the details of their lives, emotionally, physically. If I didn't have the lunches to make, the homework to do, the parties to drive them to, the beds to make, the stories to read, the fights to stop, the laundry, the floors, the games to play, the feelings to mend, the lives to shape. But the thought was brief.

Such a thought seems ludicrous and unforgivable. My boys are the reason I am strong. I gathered my strength for them; I gathered my strength from them.

"Are you happy today?" I said to Colin one morning.

"I'm happy a lot," was his response.

I did not end a marriage with a man who hurt me to be a crusader; I did not intend to become the spokesperson for all women who have been battered. I left because I finally opened my eyes and saw that the merry-go-round of abuse and eternal reconciliation would forever damn my life. It would not stop and let me off.

I saw at thirty-seven that I was doomed to give my children an image of home that was poisoned with strife. I saw that I was too young and too hopeful to be waiting for the next time. There would always be a next time. I knew that now.

He will never change. The therapist was right. The stranger at the beach knew better than me. They could both see.

I could no longer compartmentalize myself for the times in-between, when he would go to fund-raising events and tell my friends how wonderful I was and how much he didn't deserve me. He was right about that. And my children deserved a father who wasn't a reluctant passenger on family outings. At the very least, they deserved to have one parent desperate to please them, a parent who groped for the joy they brought. Me.

I could no longer tolerate a black rhino of a man who was so unpredictable in his attacks that his presence in a room made me feel strangled. The good times would never be good enough. I deserved more. My boys deserved more.

I was accomplished, I was good at what I did, I was a good person. I needed to get back to that. I needed to surround myself with friends who were affirming and focused on tomorrow. I didn't want to spend time with people who were negative and wanted to damn their husbands or the whole gender. It is not men I hate. It is not even him I hate.

This was a man I just did not know. I deplored what he did. And I despise that he did not accept responsibility for it, that he discarded a family as easily as some people toss newspapers into a recycling bin. But I do not hate him. I just wanted him to stop the hurt, the wounding in all its forms. I just wanted to recover, as I had with my appendectomy. But now the wound was even deeper, the price more severe.

I read a dozen books in the first several months after he left about abuse, recovery, and self-affirmation. My friend Dana sent me a few, and Jan, and my mom. I relished the gifts, and they helped me. I wanted to know that I was not alone, that I was not crazy, and that there was a way out, a way to feel better. I embraced stories of friends and friends of friends who left abusive marriages and changed their lives; many remarried to good men. I tried not to let the anger consume me. I wanted to feel it, but conquer it, grow past it. I did not want to become bitter and cold, hateful and vengeful. I just wanted to heal.

One woman I knew left an abusive marriage and became a downhill skier. *How appropriate, I thought, that this woman once made timid and afraid by a violent husband could now be so bold.* I liked stories about self-salvation. I wanted to have one of them. I not only wanted to get past all this, I wanted to get above it. I wanted to be better than I was before any of this happened.

I started soliciting groups where I could give speeches about parenting, about the humor in daily life. Now, instead of drowning out the noise of his negativity, the applause and the laughter from an auditorium of strangers was helping me regain the sense of who I was, of who I was alone. It was me out there making these people laugh and feel; me with my words, touching their lives, sharing with them. It was me alone at the podium. It was me.

On every ride home from every speech, usually navigating directions in a suburb I had never visited, I was euphoric, relieved that for an hour I did not have to be an abused woman. I could be just a woman, a mother, a writer, a speaker.

I used to want so much just to be ordinary, untouched by the strangeness, the hurt, the violence. I would look out at the faces of the women who came to hear me speak at parenting groups, women's groups, civic groups, and I would think, "I want your life."

Holding their babies with wedding-ringed hands, laughing, drinking coffee, making jokes—the women in the audiences seemed so content, so full. I would make them laugh and entertain them for an hour, and afterward they would come up to me and tell me how my words were so inspiring. Many women told me how much they envied me. And then I would think, well, maybe being me is okay. *If these women respect me, maybe I am okay. Maybe I will survive. Maybe I am as special as I try to convince myself.*

And maybe being a woman with my past is not so extraordinary, not so unusual, not so terrible. Maybe some of these women, with beautiful faces and shining futures, escaped like me. Maybe they will escape. Maybe their best friends are like me, maybe their sisters. But this is who I am. I was hurt, but I am still here. And I am good.

That small thought, *Okay, this is who I am, this is my past,* is empowering. Accepting yourself, and all that has happened to you, is the germination of the unfaltering, tireless strength necessary to rebuild a life without regret and negativity, without the suffocation of remorse.

"Write it all down," my mother told me. "Tell it all."

And I did, the words falling from me, my unleashed fingers typing what I dared not see or say for years, my voice given back. *He cannot take away the truth. He cannot silence me. I will speak out, and I will write it all down. What happened will not go away by pretending it didn't happen. I will grow strong by telling the truth and not running away from it.*

In the months after he left, I applied to seventeen local community colleges, junior colleges, and universities to teach journalism. With eighteen years of experience writing for newspapers and magazines and with a master's degree in journalism, I felt qualified to tell students how to write a story. And I needed to earn more to support the boys and myself.

The process of applying for teaching jobs forced me to tell over and over again, to strangers, what I was convincing myself was true. I was a solid journalist, a good writer, a competent woman. I was reminding myself who I was, and I remembered that I had done this before. When I graduated from Northwestern University in 1979, with a master's in journalism and unrestrained moxie, I sent out 117 letters and resumes to newspapers and magazines across the country. Now I was remembering the confident young woman I was before I was his wife, and I realized I am still young. There is still tomorrow.

They can't all say no.

A dean in the undergraduate program of Northwestern University called me only weeks after I sent the letter. I later interviewed for a position as an adjunct instructor in the graduate program. In June 1996, I began teaching at a place I loved and revered as a student. I have been teaching every quarter since.

That following June was my first graduation ceremony as an instructor. On that still, hot Saturday afternoon, two years after our last day at the beach as a family of five and only a block away, I sat on the stage of the auditorium. Dressed in a black robe with a purple and gold hood, I smiled as a parade of young men and women clicked across the polished wooden stage in shoes that looked new for the occasion.

The students smiled and nodded when handed their slim purple boxes, as their parents and friends erupted in forbidden applause, one year after my first day before them on the third floor of Fisk Hall. Here were the students whose names I struggled to remember the first day, the students whose names, faces, and futures I never want to forget. These students helped me, by their very presence in class, forget where I had been and remember who I was.

"She was mine," another professor whispered to me when a student was awarded a special honor. All of us—adjunct faculty, associate professors, and deans—were claiming responsibility for the young women and men as the cameras whirred and the video cameras silently hummed. The pomp, the circumstance, the odd-shaped, tasseled mortarboards flat and peculiar on our foreheads, it was a glorious circus of tradition and ceremony.

In the young women's eyes I saw myself, carrying in my own young eyes tomorrows filled with light. Eighteen years earlier, I had received the same degree in a similar ceremony in robes I remember to be the same. Each young woman I saw that June 1997 reminded me of how it felt to be twenty-one and powerfully confident, spilling an enthusiasm for living and working, trying so hard, convinced that every dream can happen, that forging a fantasy only takes time. I never want to be that young again—it is too exhausting—but I wanted to snatch their contagious spirit, a spirit at once bold and unsure, writing the rules while the game is played. This was before anything bad had happened. And I believed nothing ever would.

The shining young men I had taught gave me hope. *So this is what it will be like when my boys are no longer small enough to carry, when the past we have shared is faded and the pain they felt is muted and distant.* The young men in the classroom every quarter made me feel a part of the love their parents gave to them, made me feel hope for the love I gave my own sons. *So this is how it works. The little boys become men: men who do well and work hard, earn diplomas, meet girlfriends, and one day fill shoes larger than their fathers'. They become good men, maybe even better men.*

On that June day I was fourteen years away from Weldon's college graduation, and nineteen years from Colin's walk across a stage for a diploma. But on this Saturday I was in the middle of the time line, looking the same distance back as I was looking ahead, as far from my own moment of recognition as I was from recognizing my sons'.

I felt strong again.

I slowly began to replace thinking from a position of dread into a frame of mind of positive anticipation. I had to retrain myself not to think, *Oh, God, what will he do next?* to *What will I do next?*

Breaking away from the trap of building a life around someone's actions or moods into building a life to suit a plan, to fit a goal, a vision, takes a different kind of discipline. It takes energy every day to convince yourself you are wonderful when someone you loved and trusted denigrated you, harmed you, and left you and your family.

I began to think that my success would be the most powerful result of this heartbreak. And I began to see how I could inch toward that success, one story at a time, or even one day at a time, when I had the energy to read and tell stories to the boys, instead of collapsing after dinner and baths and homework.

"Please make Mommy laugh again." Brendan told his Sunday school teacher this was his one prayer for Christmas, that first Christmas after his father left.

I prayed for the same. And I tried to make a life for myself, for all of us, that opened to laughter.

Card received on May 30, 1989

Michele,

I'm so happy you've stayed with our love, despite your feelings of isolation and frustration. I felt the pain of your sorrow last night and I'm using it to bring me back on course with my true love for you.

Let's have fun and love each other.

Your dearest friend.

17

Letting Go of Fear

Patrick was my favorite. His voice was soothing, yet intensely insightful. When I called him weekly, I trusted he knew everything about me, even though we had never met and he had never heard my voice, and he didn't know my name. Patrick knew everything else.

Patrick was a 900-number astrologer, a weekly changing recording in a wise, dramatic British accent. I found him in a magazine, and I liked him better than the women whose numbers I called, the women with hokey names. For several months I needed Patrick as much as I needed to pray, worry, and trust that the waves in my life would eventually settle to a comfortable flow. I wanted a quiet cadence, predictable and calm. Until then, I could believe in the simple words Patrick said out loud, and when I had questions, he answered them without hearing them.

All I really wanted to know was that this whole deal was going to turn out okay, that my children would be fine, that I would be fine, that we could walk away from the bomb all in one piece. I needed to believe that I could end an abusive marriage and not only survive, but thrive. Spread my wings and be someone new. I wanted to watch the last scene where there is complete resolution and the music swells and the credits roll. I wanted someone to tell me in concrete terms that this story—my story—would have a happy ending. And I would let myself call and spend the $1.95 a minute once a week to hear it.

The fear I had about the future was ignited when I acknowledged the severity of what had happened. "Are the boys going to be a mess?" I asked a woman friend, only months after my husband left and I spent my days frenzied, working, worrying, driving them to therapy, to school, to sports, to friends' houses, anywhere I could take them to make them better. To make me better.

"My father killed himself on Christmas when I was six," my friend said flatly. "Do I seem messed up to you?"

I guess my fears were born of my ignorance and privilege. I had been blessed with a life without suffering. I was healthy; I knew I would never starve. No matter what, my family would help me. My basic needs—my boys' basic needs—would always be answered.

Before this, I had not experienced voluntary chaos. I was accustomed to the belief that the tragedies that happened in a family were caused by outside influences beyond your control: the basement flooding, losing a job, a child getting sick, relatives and friends hurt in accidents, bacteria in the restaurant food, tornadoes, a drunk driver swerving, or a tree falling through the roof. These were things you coped with, and these were the only tragedies possible. Everyone else behaved as they were expected to, out of love and respect and responsibility. If life held surprises, they were surprises that weren't anyone's fault. They were surprises life handed you just because life handed out surprises sometimes.

I had no concept of how to cope with the fallout when it resulted from behavior that wasn't accidental—elective misery. I had never known anyone to make that choice. No one would hurt you on purpose. No one intentionally created havoc, not on their own family, not deliberately.

I didn't have an inkling how to fix lives when the problems were manufactured. You don't open the window and have an abusive marriage land on you. No one forced my ex-husband to act violently. Who would choose to destroy a family, to crucify the hope in small children? Why cause your own problems when life was so uncertain anyway? Why create your own pain?

And because I viewed the violence as an unnecessary choice and as the voluntary decision of my ex-husband, I was furious, I was terrified. I was afraid of the consequence of not only everything he had done, but everything I had done. I was afraid that what I *hadn't* done had hurt my children.

While he was with us and after he was gone, fear was as much a part of my life as brushing my teeth.

It seems so silly now, but calling that stupid 900 number once a week, on Sunday night when the recording changed for the new week, helped me keep my fears at bay. "Finances look good," I would repeat to myself. "Caution is called for later in the week," I would remember. Patrick told me so. Patrick said nothing about my life being ruined—a shambles, for goodness sake—and he didn't even mention the children. If they were at risk, though, he would have mentioned it. I know.

This dependence on astrologers revealing the future did not supplant my faith. I still prayed every day, begging for help. I needed patience to raise the boys; I needed guidance to raise them alone. I needed to help them heal; I needed to know what was right for them. But for all my tearful prayers at the end of the day asking for help and reassurance, the result I got was at the expense of a toll call. Praying was calming, but Patrick talked back. He was respite from my fear, like a hot bath, like a daydream.

I once paid to have my runes read in Dallas when we lived there, by a round John Candy kind of man with a gray beard and an earthy scent. After much ruminating, he told me I may need a new prescription soon for my contacts. What I wanted to know then, back in 1984 or 1985, was whether I would have children and when. And if I would live happily ever after. If the man that I loved was the right one.

If he had told me that day that the man I was set to marry would eventually abuse me physically and emotionally, cost me more stress, emotion, self-esteem, and money than I thought possible, I think I would have walked the other way. He wasn't that good looking. He wasn't that good of a dancer. But maybe it would have made no difference. Maybe it was not something I would have heard or believed. After all, the source was just a guy in a booth at a festival reading old stones.

In 1985 I interviewed a popular psychic for a profile story. He was an Indian man who called himself a doctor, who told me as soon as we met that I had the number four on my forehead, because I was the fourth daughter in my family. He also told me that the person I loved could break my heart someday, and I would cry tears of blood. That was in 1985. I thought he was strange, and besides, the credentials he gave for his education didn't pan out. My editor killed the story because no one had heard of him at the school where he said he received his degrees.

But on my way out of the interview, the doctor gave me mantra-like phrases to repeat over and over in the mirror so it wouldn't happen, I wouldn't have my heart broken. What the heck? I did it. A year later we got married, and four months after our wedding, my husband hit me for the first time. Ten years after I met that doctor, I was crying tears of blood.

My sister Madeleine hired a psychic once for my birthday party in 1996, and even though the psychic got lost on the way to her house and stayed in the bathroom for an hour when she finally arrived, she did show me on my palm that my marriage had ended. The proclamation was without prompting from me, of course. I think I might have cried when she told me. But she assured me that in about a half-inch or so I would be bonded with my soul mate for life. Just how long a time is it between this line and that line that goes all the way around my hand? She could not be specific, and it was time for the next person in line. *Damn. Maybe Patrick knows.*

In May 1988, when I was four months pregnant with Weldon, I had my astrological chart read by a woman who served coffee and cookies with her readings. I was writing a story about some groups in Dallas that were convinced a certain alignment in the heavens was causing a global phenomenon. My due date was October 25, and this woman told me matter-of-factly that no, no, no, my son—oh, yes, it was definitely a boy—would be born October 6. She told me my son and I would be very close and he would be artistic, an old soul. A month later I was diagnosed with toxemia, and because of my high blood pressure, I was induced on October 5. Weldon was born at 4 A.M. on October 6. It was eerie.

Was it a coincidence? And why didn't she happen to mention just what was going to go down on July 1, 1995, the night I opened my eyes and my life changed?

Do I think it was all fate? No. I had a choice, as did my husband. I did not have to stay, though I did for a thousand reasons, all of which don't seem to count now. And I was brave enough to leave, finally, though I am not always brave enough to leave the fear behind. The fear served me; it kept me connected and contained. It kept me from venturing out into the world, from leaving him and all of the violence behind.

For more than two years after he left, I feared him and his behavior, though the intensity was waning. Incrementally, the fear would leave me, and each piece I had to push away. Some days when he came for visitation, I would not be afraid when his car pulled into the driveway. My heart would not pound when he stepped out to greet the boys. Still, I could not relax when he had them on a visitation, afraid that if I did, something would happen. If I worried from 10 A.M. to 6 P.M. Saturday when he was with one of my sons, then my fear would protect that child. And if I lived my life feeling like the girl in the B movie waiting for the bogeyman to strike in the window, at least the fear would be my companion. I would not be alone.

Fear is a funny thing. You can become afraid of not being afraid, because the fear is so familiar. I was afraid of the man I had married, afraid he would appear somewhere, afraid he would ruin our plans. I was always afraid.

He still controlled part of my life that way.

On the last day of the group sessions I attended at Sarah's Inn in 1995, the other women in the group and I performed a letting-go ceremony. It was a December night, cold, brittle, a brisk wind whipping through the yard of the building. We had blown up brightly colored balloons and written on them in markers what we wanted to release, what we wanted expunged from our lives. I wrote his name on mine and I also wrote "fear." We were encouraged to forgive. That part I faked.

We went out the back door, down the stairs off the porch. We sang a song and said some words we had written together. Then we released our balloons into the ink-dark night. Most of the other women were crying. I was going through the motions; I had let go of the string, but the fear was with me as much as the mole on my back and the freckles on my face.

The fear stayed with me for almost another two years. One night I realized it was time to begin letting it go. I had no need for the fear anymore; it no longer served me. It was the night of the explosion.

Colin was the first in the tub filling with bubbles, the white-foamed water covering him to the middle of his chest. "Put your feet in, Mom!" he coaxed, as Brendan jumped to claim his space in the back, where he would hold court with Spiderman, a killer whale, a Tazmanian Devil, and a red Batman missing a hand. Weldon was the last in and maneuvered to the front, staking his rightful place in the kingdom of the tub as the oldest, controller of the faucet and the shampoo.

This was their evening ritual and one they refused to outgrow: a raucous bath together after dinner, covering the tile floor with a half-inch of water as they poked and boasted and dove. They always laughed as Colin proclaimed, "I'm a shark!" gasping to hold his breath before going head-first into the bubbles.

I was doing what I did every night, my mental to-do list, my mapping of the evening's tasks, how to get them dressed and read to, their homework organized, the laundry done, my papers graded, our clothes put away before collapsing. I kept this ritual checklist of our lives as if staying organized kept my demons at bay. The phone rang—it was my mother—and as I watched a condensed, waterlogged game of tag in the tub, we talked about our days.

Then we heard it: a sonic boom, an earthquake, a collision, a near-deafening, exaggerated cartoon-like sound, something out of the movie *Space Jam* or a Road Runner rerun. The house jolted, then rocked back, followed by glass shattering, clanking, and falling, so close and so loud, I had to check the bathroom window and the mirror to make sure whatever happened was not in the same room as us.

What is he doing to us now?

Then there was silence. No war screams, no shouting from outside. The boys, wide-eyed and afraid, sat still in the bathtub, quiet as fish.

Phone in my hand, my heart pounding, I asked my mother, "What happened?" as if she would know and be able to fix it all, as she always had done. "My house shook too," she said from her home four blocks away. "I'll call the police."

I jumped down the stairs two at a time, barefoot, telling the boys to stay upstairs and get dried and dressed. Five of the first-floor windows were blown in—living room, dining room—daggers of glass had blown as far as ten feet across the rooms, glistening on the floor, the furniture, the rug. Everywhere silver pieces shimmered from the light in the hall. The wind blew through the empty window frames.

I stopped, startled. We had been right there, my boys and I, just moments earlier. They'd been running in circles and squealing while I rounded them upstairs; now shards of windows littered every step. In a flash I saw what could have been, something beyond my control.

It was that feeling you get in the center of you—more in your soul than in your stomach, more in your very self than in your heart—that feeling you get when you swerve the car avoiding an accident or you hear the news of a friend's child suddenly sick, hurt, or worse, and you know you have been salvaged from a random tragedy. In my soul I saw my laughing, quixotic boys, covered in glass razors, bleeding. I felt the blood rush from my head, my mouth went dry, and my legs and feet went numb.

No matter what had happened to them until that moment, I knew I could have lost my boys that night. And I hadn't prepared to be afraid of an explosion. I didn't know that day that I should have been afraid of feeling safe inside my own house.

Over the course of that long night, I learned that an empty home across the street from ours exploded from an apparent gas leak from an appliance. At least a dozen homes were damaged on our block, and damaged cars, roofs, windows, and garages, all part of the property damage toll beyond the $1 million mark.

But no one was hurt.

Thankfully, gratefully, miraculously, on one of the first warm April evenings of the year, my sons were exhausted from playing outside for hours and were in the bathtub earlier than usual. We were not downstairs. The white brick house across the street was gone, but I mourned no one.

Over the next few weeks, as the gapers and curious gawked and pointed and begged the story to be retold, I could not muster any emotion but gratitude. When a friend called it a tragedy, I shrugged. We lost things, not each other. This is nothing like we've had to recover from. I only had to sweep, vacuum, pick up glass, make phone calls, and wait for tradespeople to do what they intended. We were only inconvenienced.

I thought back to who I was before I was a single mother, before I was forced to brace myself for the deliberate explosions aimed at me, that were far more deleterious, far more damaging than the one that shattered our windows that night. I had known how to be afraid of someone who loved me, someone who was supposed to be safe.

I have learned that I cannot stop the explosions, not from a house across the street, not from my ex-husband's puzzling darkness, not from his unpredictable behavior. I cannot even promise myself or my boys there will be no more. Nothing is as simple as I had thought, growing up in my safe house, with my loving family, living my protected life where bad things happened by accident.

When I married the charming young boy I knew my whole life, the Catholic boy everyone thought was wonderful, I could not have predicted or stopped the violence any more than I could have predicted or stopped the house across the street from exploding in the night, scaring my boys in the bathtub.

The fear has been leaving me in increments since that night, and I feel full and unburdened at times—vignettes that are pure and without the poison of vigilance. It is a light feeling, of weightlessness, not carelessness, but a kind of euphoria, without the patches of darkness creeping into my view. Sometimes I don't remember to be afraid, and sometimes I feel I don't have to, like when we are together in my sister Madeleine's house in Michigan or we are driving home from an adventure and the boys are sleeping, cool and happy. I can live in the moment and embrace the joy of the day, relish the gift of the life we have.

And then comes a phone call or a letter from an attorney calling me back to my fear, and I think: If I am afraid, will I have truly won? In the last few years since he left there have been pure moments when I am living without fear, when I am happy and focused on the good and the positive, not worried or encumbered by what may happen. I try to stay there, but it's hard.

When I lose faith in my own power and falter, getting drawn back to the magnet of fear, I feel that I must concentrate to regain my strength and do what needs to be done. It is then that I focus on what I must do, and that is to care for me and care for my boys, working around the fears of the past and my fears for our future.

I am still letting go of the fear. I have learned that without it, the explosions still come, the hurt still happens; I only lose less of my life waiting for it. And I have learned that whatever comes to our house, whatever comes in our lives, I will bend with it. I can withstand the explosions, and I will not break.

Card received on April 10, 1995

Colin delivered this a little early. I believe our lives have entered a new stage with Weldon's T-ball, the shuttling parents stage. It will be more difficult, but because we are now communicating and working daily on our relationship, these new demands will be easy.

And when things get crazy, we can always recline on our new patio.

I love our relationship and life together. Let's keep working.

18

What Do You Know to Be True?

I don't gossip anymore. My last few years starring in community chatter has made me a changed woman. In one day I went from being the writer who lives in that house over there with her three boys and her attorney husband to the battered woman, abandoned, pathetic. With one emergency order of protection, I went from the person people talked to, to a person people talked about. About someone else's problems, my lips are now sealed.

The line Olympia Dukakis drawled in *Steel Magnolias*—"If you don't have anything nice to say about somebody, sit next to me"— no longer makes me giggle; it makes me squirm. I have been the gossipee in barge loads of local gossip—some embellished, some flat-out wrong, one heck of a lot of it true—and all of it hurt. There have been times when varying versions of my life were repeated to me so often that the words "I heard that you" would cause a Pavlovian response of tears welling in my eyes and my heart pounding in my chest before the tail end of the gossip ever hit. I wanted to be anonymous. I wanted to hide. I'm not kidding myself that a lot of these men and women talking about my life were truly concerned about my welfare. I was just a juicy story. A continuing juicy story.

Women whose names I couldn't remember but whose van license plates I recognized from carpool lines at preschools, grade schools, and recreation centers would console me on my most recent translated disaster or congratulate me on my latest passed-on triumph, all of which was third- and fourth-hand, and none of which came from my lips to their ears. I was living in flesh and full color that hysterically entertaining kindergarten game of telephone when "I ate a cheeseburger yesterday" turns into "I hate the jeans Bernie wore today" by the time the sentence reaches the last kid in the last row. But as a grown woman with a fleeting sense of dignity, I no longer found it funny.

One afternoon I ran into a woman I knew at Kinko's who told me (she had gotten it from a friend of a friend of a friend) that after I threw my poor husband out of the house, he was not allowed to come home, even though he was contrite and repentant, and that actually I was the aggressor and he was too ashamed to say so, you know, being a champion boxer and all. I barked, I waved, I flailed, I may have even shown her the affidavit of abuse I was at Kinko's to copy anyway. Needless to say, this woman has not spoken to me since. I wager she has spoken about me though.

Another woman told my friend Ellen that she knew my former husband from college, so I must be making all this up. And when he got remarried seven months after our divorce and had a child nine months later, it was a gossiper's field day.

I was not so vainglorious or conceited to think I was the topic of cocktail party conversations in every living room across town. But it was news, big news, two locals with a soap-opera story. The perfect couple wasn't. *Did you hear?*

I felt brave enough finally acknowledging publicly—if only to lawyers and judges and people who knew me well—that my handsome lawyer husband abused me. But it gave me the creeps that elaborately augmented stories and dangerously false versions of my autobiography were passed around like the collection basket at church. I was tired of walking into a room and having it suddenly grow hushed. I was tired of explaining and apologizing. I was sick of starring in the tabloid story.

Just as the bully on the playground who gets pushed down for the first time realizes, "Aw, gee, this stinks," I will no longer wag my tongue about others known and unknown, no matter what life's lesson may justify the tale. I have learned the hard way not to wonder for whom the tongue wags; it wags for thee.

I am done telling tales out of school. I was never truly malicious, but I was a weekly gossip columnist for the *Dallas Times Herald* at one heady point of my life, and God, it was fun. I learned Dionne Warwick was as insistent about raspberry Jell-O as Joan Crawford was about wire hangers. I learned firsthand that Jerry Hall's language could make Courtney Love blush, and that in person, Rod Stewart looked his age. I learned that Tom Cruise was one of the nicest human beings I ever met and that Gloria Steinem carried lipstick in her purse.

I wrote about famous people for work, and I brought my work home and talked about everybody else. And I had enablers. There were my growing-up friends, my high school friends, my college friends, my Texas friends, my downtown friends, my teaching friends, my family friends, and oh, yes, my sisters, who had their own network of friends. All of them contributed to my regular devouring of insider information that was on some level probably illegal, if not immoral and just plain unkind.

As I look back on my years of gossipmongering, I wonder what it ever really did for me. I guess I was hoping that by repeating these stories of lousy husbands, financial crises, or sudden illnesses out loud, I could be spared a similar heartache. Just as if saying "bunny, bunny" on the first day of the month, knocking on wood, or calling your mother every day could make you immune to any ill that may befall you.

And then my life tore at the seams. I had to admit, out loud, that the man I married hurt me deliberately. Now there's something to talk about.

But I learned through the cruel path of idle chatter that at any point, something awful could happen to good people—like me, like you, like anyone. It makes no sense, and all of it gets confused and garbled in the translation. I have learned by living publicly through the fallout of the abuse that most people's lives are a muddy place, and that in any given sweeps season, Lindsay Wagner or Meredith Baxter could portray your life in a mini-series and get decent ratings.

I don't talk trash anymore. I have been dragged through the mud no matter how hard I tried to transcend it. And the truth about my personal life was always far worse than anybody's fiction.

But that's not why I write about it. I write to heal and to explain it to myself. I write to give witness to what happened, to take control over the life I lost control of. I write to name the abuse and erode the shame, to claim responsibility for my role. I write to get the poison, the weight, the hurt out of my body. I write to set myself free, to validate what is true.

"What do you know to be true?" I ask the boys when they question the past or even when someone on the playground tells a fib or concocts a wild story. Usually they stammer a little, but I can almost see them searching inside, the modem clicking into the Internet. And they come up with it every time. I want them to rely on themselves and have the confidence to believe the truth, their truth, no matter who vehemently denies it.

"It's raining," my therapist said to me. "Don't let anyone tell you it's not." When I was married, when I was abused, it was raining and I was wet and cold. Even if he tried his damnedest to convince me the sun was shining, it was raining—raining hard.

What do you know to be true? It calls me back to myself.

Without prompting, Weldon says he remembers the screaming and crying, the videotape where Mommy's face is puffy. He says he remembers the tears I shed and that the reasons I gave for them were strange. Brendan told anyone who listened for months after my ex-husband left that he would never hit his wife when he grew up. He told anyone who came to our house that he would be a good dad and love the mommy. Colin told his preschool teachers that Daddy punched Mommy and he lives somewhere else now.

It hurts to hear your children say those words. But it is much more hurtful to deny to them what they know to be true and not give them the space to say what they know. It is blinding to come out, to admit what has happened. I didn't have a glamorous story to announce. I wasn't admitting to a secret ten-year affair with John Kennedy Jr. or claiming Brad Pitt was the father of my quintuplets. It's not exciting or enviable to say you were battered. It's comparable to saying you have some highly contagious disease, one that is scornful, misunderstood, and filled with myth and shame.

But it doesn't have to be that way. If I tell the truth, then perhaps it will help to dissolve the myths about abuse: that battered women ask for it, that they are familiar with violence, that they don't want to leave the abuse, that it was somehow their fault. None of those things were true for me or any of the women I met at Sarah's Inn. Popular beliefs and myths can be rewritten, reshaped, reborn. It takes telling the truth, the undeniable, indisputable truth to change false notions. If it wasn't possible, we would still believe the Earth is flat.

The most important thing I can do now is be honest to myself and to my boys. And it feels crucial for me to keep telling and keep writing so my truth and the truth of millions of women like me does not get lost in misconceptions. The gift I give to my boys and myself is the honest account of how and why this happened in our lives and how I could have possibly allowed it, how I stopped it all, and how we survived.

"The truth won't hurt them, lies will," my friend Alison told me when I first started writing it all down.

I hope the lesson I leave my boys and anyone who will hear me is that when something terrible happens, even something humiliating, you don't deny it, you change from it. I took this chunk of my life and created something lasting, something I hope will be useful. Some women paint, others sew, some run, garden, or master a skill. Still others hold their pain inside them, hoping it will not leak all over the carpets and the new furniture in the middle of the Christmas party with all the relatives present.

I write.

What do you know to be true?

I was a battered wife. I am not anymore. I will never be again.

I have found that when you allow truth into your life, it leaves space for strength to emerge and grow, replacing shame and making it unnecessary to hide. The strength was always there, and the telling empowers you to employ it.

I am proud to tell this story. I know it to be true.

Card received on June 5, 1992

Michele,

You are such a wonderful wife and mother. I will always be at your side. This baby [in the card] is almost as beautiful as our baby Brendan, but I really felt attracted to the baby duck at the infant's side. It reminded me of the Pet Parade. Maybe next year we can be in the Pet Parade.

This card comes at a time of great hope for you. Writing for the Chicago Tribune *is a step up from Dallas. This one looks like a winner because you know what they want and what they want is your immense ability. Again, we must wait for your book—that will work—but I know how disappointed you must feel. Stay with it. I have not met your match in God-given ability. You will flourish using it.*

So my dear love, Happy Birthday. I love you more than I ever have. You are as beautiful as you ever were, and we have the two beautiful manifestations of our love.

Love.

19

Double Parent

The label doesn't fit. The job description falls short. So I want—officially and emphatically—to request a name change for every parent who raises children without a spouse or partner. From this day forward, let us retire the current misnomer of Single Parent for the more accurate Double Parent.

I was single once, and though I am technically single again, there is no similarity between my life as an unmarried, childless twenty-five-year-old who was clueless and idealistic to boot and my life as a forty-year-old with three lives in my hands and an uncooperative ex-husband on the other end of the phone. I don't even wear the same kind of earrings or shoes.

Every day I am a double parent. There is nothing singular about anything I do, not even when I take a shower and two or three pairs of hands tug at the shower curtain, encouraging me to hurry.

A double parent does duty on everything from baseball games, homework, and storytelling to runny noses, upset stomachs, play dates, sheet changing, doctor visits, chicken pox, and recovery from the kids who push on the playground. We do it well, we do it without help, we do a lot of it with knots in our throats and pains in our stomachs. We do it wishing it was another way and trying to remember that millions of women, throughout the history of the world, have done this very same thing all by themselves. Widowed, divorced, left alone, even choosing the option, women have always been raising children alone, children who grow up to be good men and women.

Why does it feel so hard sometimes?

One recent weekend Brendan had a team picture at 8:15 A.M., followed by Weldon's doctor appointment at 9:00, Brendan's T-ball game at 9:30, Weldon's team picture at 10:30, followed by his baseball game at 11:30. And Colin? I prayed that he would not get a concussion as I chased him across two separate diamonds and a doctor's office. I don't want to go into details about the month when they all suffered through chicken pox, passing it from one to the next until each of them was covered in varying stages of red, oozing sores in utter agony.

I get through it all telling myself I didn't lose a helpful partner. Though my Daddy Envy was intense, if I look at the past truthfully, I didn't lose the kind of partner I always wanted as a father for my children. I didn't lose the kind of daddy I needed to envy. I lost a liability. I spent more energy crying and recovering with him in the house than I do occasionally feeling sorry for myself that I do it alone.

Before he left our home for good, he was gone most every day of the week, whether as a law student studying, working, and contributing as the editor of the law review, or as a new attorney in a firm that required a high total of billable hours. And when he was home, he was tired, withdrawn. He wasn't really there.

In the years when their father was in our home, I didn't look at our family honestly. The fantasy of a complete, happy family that I conjured compelled me to stay with a man who hit me. I looked at the Christmas snapshots of us posed by the tree and told myself it would all be fine. *We can be as we look in the pictures,* I thought, truly believing that all you had to do was wish upon a star to make it so. *All the wishes could erase the menace,* I thought. *We must stay a family. No matter what.*

And for years, it worked. I rationalized it all, absorbing my boys and their joy, concentrating on their needs, and ignoring what he was doing to me. I also knew in my heart that eventually I would hit a wall. There would come a day when I would stop pretending it was perfect, wishing it would change, mourning what never was and realize that with my husband gone, I lost less than I won.

I gained the joy of three children growing up in a house without explosive conflict, a land mine of emotions, a house without pain. In our house, as the only adult, I get to hear it all, feel it all, see it all. There is no one else to share it with, but it does not diminish its worth—it doubles the dividend. Most of it all is good.

"I'm kind of magical," Brendan whispered to me one afternoon as I was writing on my office computer. "Close your eyes and you'll see," he said as he planted a kiss on my cheek, running off to his room, laughing and shouting. It felt twice as good.

"You're my happy thought," Weldon told me once after watching the movie *Hook*. And being the only one to hear it, my joy doubled.

"Hi, chickens!" Colin used to shout out the window to the birds gathered on the front lawn in the morning. Mostly he relished the sound of his own voice reaching the trees and beyond. I was the only parent there, so my heart swelled to twice the size.

I have changed. I have these children. They are why I am here.

Being a mother alone is much harder than I ever imagined. It is more maddening, but less mad and more sane than anything I have ever done. It makes sense. It is pure. It stretches me to levels of patience I never imagined and depths of humility I never wanted to reach. It is better to be honest as a mother than to drown in your own wishes.

"I need the song," Colin sniffled through tears as he came into my room late one night after a bad dream. With one song sung in whispers—his favorite bedtime song—he fell fast asleep, collapsing like a load of folded laundry, warm from the dryer, smelling fresh and sweet and new.

Most early mornings (even without bad dreams), Colin scampers into my room, sometimes it's after 2:00, sometimes just before 5:00, and jumps into my bed. He hurries to get under the covers and calls my white cotton-comfortered bed the cloud bed. "Let's get under the clouds, Momma," he says.

If they didn't squirm and fight and jostle, I could hold them all day. Right after their bath, their hair smells fruity and clean, flush to their heads, combed neatly, the rows of their blond hair as neat as cornfields, freshly planted. Their skin is flushed, their cotton pajama shirts are tender, and they are smiling. I swear at those times I forget everything bad that has ever happened. I want them to forget too.

I plan their birthday parties for months, and I try so hard to make them memorable, too hard sometimes, because I'm trying to edge out, replace any memory that hurts them. I want them to remember laughter, and I want the laughter to drown out old tears.

"I love you six hundred," Colin said one day.

"I love you to Pluto and back again," Brendan said.

"I love you more than anyone has ever loved anyone," Weldon responded.

"I love you to the garage and back," Colin said, not to be out-done.

Weldon is tall and gangly, with long legs like a colt's. He is kind and so smart. He loves science books, C. S. Lewis, and scary stories that he tells over and over. He likes books on airplanes and building things. He can spend hours concocting machinery and spaceships from Lego building blocks. He is a good friend and is gentle when he is not pretending to be tough. He is fast like the wind and excels in sports like his father.

When he was seven, he put four wheels on the bottom of a plastic laundry basket so I could just push it along the floor with my feet. "It'll help you, Mom," he said, so proud of his day's work. It was quite ingenious actually: he cut holes in the bottom of the basket, measuring perfectly, placing wheels inside and securing them with a nut larger than the hole.

Brendan is a calmer soul and inhabits the world of his drawings and his cartoon characters. He is quieter, more internal. He can spend hours at his desk, drawing and coloring, making elaborate scenes and story lines. He writes books, stapling them together and reading them aloud when he is finished. Dragons, monsters, good guys, knights, all star in his dramas. "There was a queen and three princes," his story began one night. "And the middle prince was so special."

Pale and peach-toned, he is handsome and cherubic. Brendan brought his tattered, tag-less Beanie Baby collection in a large basket to his Cub Scouts induction. He explained each purchase and why he received it. "This was when I was sick," he told anyone who would listen. "This was when I was sad," he explained further.

"I'm home now!" Colin calls when he returns home from preschool on the days I am in my office at home writing. "I've been gone a long time and I have a lot of things to tell!" he teases from downstairs. "I made you important things!" I display his "hard work" of stapling and stamping, his finger paintings, his sculptures of toothpicks and colored foam popcorn. "This is an important thing!" he calls until I emerge.

Colin is sweet and mischievous, his white blond hair flat and smooth, his blue eyes not almond shaped like Brendan's, but rounded. He is mercurial, quick to learn to ride his bike, quick to learn to shoot baskets in the backyard, quick to learn his alphabet, and the first to laugh at any family dinner.

I remember it all. I don't want to forget a millisecond. It is all so close I can almost touch the memories, contain them, hold them, bouncing off each other; their phrases, their looks, their wonder. I remember their laughter, their jokes, their tears, their disappointments. And when I look at them sleeping, I can't remember how loud they can be, how upset I sometimes get when they won't make their beds or stop arguing, hitting each other, or jumping on the beds and the couches.

But when I watch them sleep, it conjures a contentment I can't duplicate or derive from anything else I do, not from writing, not from creating, not from teaching, not from anything else. This is

227

Big. This is Really Big. If I do this well, this is everything. This matters, this totally matters. This is it. I have three lives in my hands, three pairs of little hands in mine. The insides of their hands are the best reasons for being a mother: so small, so hopeful, so tenacious, so trusting.

I have to do this right.

"I want to jump in the sky and grab the moon," Weldon told me one night.

"And then what will you do with it?" I asked.

"Throw it to you so we can play."

Can I love them enough by myself? Will they be okay?

For all the sorrow and guilt I feel, for the grief that festers in me for the mistakes I made, some days I feel it will all be fine. Some days I truly believe, in the center of myself, sincerely believe they will be fine, unscathed, unharmed by all of this. They will recover. They have recovered. They will grow up to be good husbands, good fathers, men who treat women with love and respect, men who are kind.

And if that happens, if my sons are okay, yes, it was worth it all. For all the years of being pulled in ten directions at once, privacy deprivation, boy cartoons, insipid videos, practices at opposite ends of town at the same time, and nights aching with exhaustion, I do have my children. I am victorious in that. I hope for them a world painted in primary colors and perfection. I hope for them the safety and assurance that someone who loves them will not hurt them. I hope for them every dream they can ever imagine. I hope they remember the good things. I hope their lives grow around the spaces where life was not joyful, where life was not perfect. I hope I served them well.

Since I landed in this role of double parent, I have had to paddle hard to overcome the feeling of drowning, of being consumed and overwhelmed by what lay ahead. I knew I didn't have the luxury of skipping a stroke; I had to keep paddling to meet all their physical needs as well as keep them feeling well-loved, content, safe, peaceful. I had to help them heal.

In the first several months after my ex-husband left the house, I had a recurring dream. In it, I was at the outdoor pool at the Lincoln Park Zoo, with the polar bears and the seals. But there were sharks in the pool too. Suddenly, a blond boy would fall into the pool, and I would dive in to rescue him, my clothes on, heavy and wet. I thought the boy was one of my sons.

Always the boy's back was turned to me, and it wasn't until I had pushed the boy to the surface for safety that I realized he was not mine. But more and more little blond boys kept falling in, and I was pushing them all to safety, only to be panicked at the realization that none were Weldon, Brendan, or Colin. I had saved other children, but I couldn't save my own.

Why can't I save my own boys? The sharks kept circling us, and I kept feeling the fear. *Yet it doesn't matter what happens to me,* I thought. I needed to keep the little boys safe. I would wake up from the dream sweating, crying, my heart pounding so hard sometimes I couldn't go back to sleep.

This is not real hard to figure out.

When I called my mother one night, feeling almost devoured by the burden of holding up the house and everyone inside it, I told her it was terrifying feeling as if my life had no safety net, as if I was always on the high wire, balancing, tottering, unable to look down, afraid to fall.

"I will be your safety net," she said without pause.

As the months and years evolved, and I have sometimes felt I succeeded in doing this alone, I realize now I was more alone when there were two parents in the house. It just didn't look that way to strangers.

I knew now that my sisters were there for the biggest and smallest things and that my brothers and their wives helped me all they could. My good friends filled in the gaps, and if the boys missed a practice once a month because I couldn't get home from work on time or be in three places at once, then they missed a practice and I apologized to the coach. I bought team snacks instead of making them from scratch and didn't always reciprocate for sleepovers when the boys were asked. We ate frozen food heated in the microwave more than I would have liked, and sometimes after a long day I lost my temper and shouted. Sometimes I didn't want to drive them to basketball practice or the baseball game, and sometimes I said so and drove them anyway because they needed to go. Sometimes I was impatient when teaching them to read or doing their addition flash cards, and many times I hoped they understood.

Some nights I put them to bed a half-hour earlier than they usually went because I needed them taken care of, I needed the night to be over so I could grade papers or meet a deadline or just have some peace. And sometimes I yelled when they wouldn't do what I asked, fought with each other, or fought with me. Sometimes I just felt so overwhelmed I wanted to sit and cry. But I always remembered to tell them I loved them, and I always remembered to start and end every day of their lives with those words and a hug. I remembered what my sister Madeleine told me: "They are not getting younger. It can only get easier."

I waded through it all, and so much of it was good, even if it was exhausting. When I look back, sometimes I don't know how I did it at all, how I got the energy, where I found the strength, but it was there. I did my best, and I prayed every day that it was enough. I swallowed my Daddy Envy when I could and eventually lost the need for it. I hoped that one parent, who would do everything she could and then some, was good enough.

"Lots of women raised children alone when their husbands died in the war," my mother reassured me. "And they turned out all right."

She is right. Children who grow up to be great successes are raised by widows and widowers, mothers who never married, and women divorced when the children were young. Millions of parents do it very well, alone. It's just that in my self-conscious pity I picture everybody else whole and happy, two parents smiling in the holiday greetings, pine garlands on the mantle. I picture that no one else has been through what I have, and my envy sabotages me. I picture everybody else the way I dreamed my family would be.

I know now that's a waste of my time.

I have a few friends who are also doing this alone, their circumstances different than mine, but with their daily lives much the same. None of us planned this part, but we are all doing the best we can. They are all strong, beautiful women who love their children without boundaries. It has to be good enough. We do it well because we can, because it is better to be alone raising children than to be raising them with a partner who is violent—no matter how captivating and convincing the family photo album is.

We do it knowing there is grace afforded to mothers like us and that the ability to take care of our children arrives and stays with us. We can do it alone. We can do it well.

At the house on Linden Avenue in Oak Park I placed hanging baskets of impatiens on the front porch each spring. One year the flowers were fuchsia and orange. The flowers were protected from the rain there, but the sun enveloped them in the gold dust of the late afternoon, and they grew bushy and wide, thick and full of deep color.

I would water them carefully every few days, reaching high with the watering can, drenching the black soil until the water ran out the bottom of the white plastic container, spilling in trickles and splashes.

The third spring in that house, I noticed that a small brown bird—I think perhaps a wren or a sparrow—was usually in the basket when I watered. She flew out immediately when she felt water pouring around her. I thought it was odd, but not being a member of the Audubon Society or knowing anything about ornithology, I assumed this bird found the flowering basket a calm, beautiful place to rest. I did not know she was building her nest inside. I didn't know this was her home for her babies.

Several weeks later the bird was inside the basket chirping and fluttering in the flowers any time I walked on the porch. So I carefully took down the basket from its hook to have a look. Inside a halo of flowers, in a sanctioned space cleared of leaves and buds, was a neatly crafted nest with three tiny birds, the size of caterpillars, as small as thimbles.

They were so new they made the tiniest bleeping sounds with their necks tilted back and their mouths open to the sky. Gaping with hunger, need, and confusion, they waited for her, their mother, the only support system they knew.

Perhaps she came to our house because she knew we had something in common. Perhaps she knew that my house was a sheltered place to land, to build a home, to feed your children, to give them all you have, to love them fiercely, and to let them fly away.

Card received on our sixth anniversary, August 23, 1992

Dearest Michele,

I believe we are entering into the stages of true love. It's a stage I liken to being "old shoes" together. It comes from time and is based on implicit trust of each other. We survived South Bend together. I was able to see your strength and commitment overcome what seemed insurmountable. (Remember I got the flu the one time I commuted to South Bend for a weekend last summer?) I was also able to see how you have stayed so lovingly committed to our children.

But this is past. Not so distant past, but past nonetheless. Now you and I both flourish in the uncharted but friendly waters. Neither of us has achieved what we have ultimately dreamed for ourselves. That will come, ironically, not from professional advancement, but from the growth of our love for each other. That love, these "old shoes" living forever, will open us up to our greatest, richest selves.

I call upon the strength of Mary and the grace of our marriage to stay completely faithful to you. I happily now renew our vow of marriage and await the true riches of our life together.

20

The Color Apricot

The color was with me for years; I even dreamed of it—a rich, creamy apricot that made me feel warm and safe and at the same time liberated and daring. I tore out magazine photographs of walls, bedspreads, even pillowcases and dresses in this peachy glow, each time feeling, "Yes, that's it," as if this particular shade was suddenly everywhere, and my yearning for it was universally endorsed. When I was in rooms painted my color, I felt centered, beautiful, independent. I forgot who I was and what my life was really like, and I concentrated on the color. I wanted to surround myself with it.

I've read enough decorating magazines and watched enough *This Old House* segments to know that color can change a room. But I was looking more for color to change my life. This one was about me.

I had bought a gallon of paint poetically titled "Guava Jam" in the spring of 1995 when I was in an adventurous mood, after toiling over color charts for several weeks before that. We were still married, and it was months before he would leave our house for good and the wounds that I had been holding together with bits of gum and sheer tenacity would spill blood for everyone to see. I was looking for distraction, change, a project to consume a month of weeknights when I didn't have to think, I could just do. He disliked my color choice and told me to leave well enough alone. Cream is fine, he said. But I planned to paint the living room my dream shade as soon as I had the chance.

But with the boys so young and omnipresent and my marriage so draining, as well as all the complications, compromises, bouts of flu, T-ball games, and dike-plugging emergencies that defined my life, that chance was not forthcoming. My gallon of paint sat in the basement workroom, unopened and unused, reminding me of my failed commitment to change.

I call this periodic urge of mine my High Visual Impact calling, and because of it I have painted entire apartments and three homes, sewn more than fifty pillows by hand, made curtains, tiled a floor, refinished furniture, and glue-gunned together more wreaths than in a church's Christmas bazaar.

In the duplex on Oram in Dallas, I plunged into my fabric mode, buying yards for curtains, tablecloths, and pillows. I also made a coffee table with two stone foo dogs I bought at a garden store with a rectangular glass top perched precariously on the heads. When we lived in South Bend, I tried so hard to make that small rented ranch house into something extravagant by painting every room, adding borders, even covering the front hall wall with fabric, that it looked more than a little like the *Green Acres* set. Eva Gabor meets Hooterville.

The house on Linden, oh, the house on Linden, where our new life would start and we'd all live happily ever after. I sponged our bedroom the palest pink over whipped ivory. I rag-rolled the dining room a high-gloss turquoise, painted the family room white, and painted the cabinets and walls of the kitchen high-gloss white. I stenciled cherries near the ceiling in the kitchen: bright red cherries, black stems, green leaves. It must have taken me nearly a month, a few hours or less at a time. Then I turned Weldon and Brendan's room into a castle of sorts, complete with a fire-breathing dragon on one wall, at Weldon's request. Brendan asked for a "nice friendly dragon." He explained, "I want the kind to play with, not the kind to eat me."

But each time I changed a room, I was only more painfully aware that I was not changing what was screaming for change. I was still married to a man who treated me in a way I couldn't tell my best friend. I was still loving a man who hit me. I was still living with the man who taunted so cruelly I could never let my sisters know. No matter how absorbed I would be in a room, in changing its look, no amount of paint or pretending could remodel his behavior.

As the months wore on and I came closer to the realization that life is designed to be joyful and not an endurance test, my apricot craving grew more difficult to ignore. Because this time painting my living room was about much more than painting my living room. It was about listening to the voice inside me and the undeniable logic that it preached. It was about taking back the reins.

Seven months after my first dance with Guava Jam at the paint store, I got my chance. It was September 1995. There was no longer someone in the house to question and criticize my choices. The man who said I was making the house look like a basket of Easter eggs was gone. I was no longer required to spend my energy in self-defense. I was no longer spending my nights dreading his key turning in the lock. I was alone with my boys in our house now and forever, and we could create for ourselves any dream we dared. I was healing.

I plotted and planned and reread my bible, *Paint Magic* by Jocasta Innes, and looked forward to the chunk of time I could finagle for the boys to be away. Their grandparents would take them for a day. This was going to be almost as great as a week at Canyon Ranch, which I could never afford. More than a long hot soak in an aromatic tub, more than a dream-filled nap, more than an afternoon of reading long-awaited books, more than an opportunity to be with close women friends, I wanted to—no, needed to—transform something. I could have done a mud mask, but totally changing a twenty-foot space was much more appealing, much more dramatic. Besides, I thought, I could write all the horrible stuff I was feeling on the walls and paint over it.

I could write on the walls.

Deep down in the transmission of my soul, I needed to make a change you could see, something that would last for years, if necessary, and be a reminder of who I really was: a woman who was not always and permanently afraid, a woman who could change. I needed to see for myself something positive that I had done, a move that was not born out of hurt, but strength, creativity.

Alone in my paint-splattered shorts and T-shirt, I took to the living room with my Guava Jam. To satisfy every longing, I denied myself the simplicity of painting with brush and roller. With dozens of different textures of rags I rubbed and rolled the paint in varying intensities, washing, smooshing and spreading my soul in every inch of wall in that room until I felt the best I had in years.

Here were the New Job, New Baby, Best Friend Visit, Surprise Birthday Party, Size Six Jeans, Cheese Soufflé, and Valentine's Day Roses feelings all rolled into one. True, this was not as grand an accomplishment as winning the Pulitzer Prize or saving the dolphins, but to a woman who was shuffling back and forth to divorce court and couldn't drive without crying, this was my Mount Everest.

This felt as significant as standing in line on July 7, 1995, in domestic violence court to end my life as a victim and start my life as a free woman. But this was definitely more aesthetically pleasing. Simpler. Cheaper.

At the end of that glorious exercise, I had a room exactly the color in my dreams. And I began steps toward making a life where my dreams are possible. The afternoon sun glowed on the walls, and I felt as if I was in the south of France in a chateau overlooking the vineyards. You could see the color from the street, and our home looked happy as you drove past. "I did that," I said to myself. I changed my life. And all it took was a lifetime and a gallon of Guava Jam.

My life after my husband left has been filled with what I call my Guava Jam moments. They help to show me that living honestly opens my life up to treasure. It's easy to feel sorry for myself: working different jobs, raising the boys alone, trying to keep it all together. But it's much more enriching to look at the times when I have done it well.

One summer night I decided to grill hamburgers outside, not an easy task with Colin trying to help. I got the coals lit and white after much fussing, Weldon helped me shuck the corn, and Brendan set the white wooden picnic bench in the backyard with plastic plates and cups. Dinner was delicious, and we laughed a lot. Afterward, the boys ran relay races from the house to the swing set and back. Then I let the empty plates sit on the porch awhile, and we all laid down in the grass, our heads near each other's.

We played a game to see who could spot the birds and airplanes first. "Bird!" you needed to call, and everyone would scan the sky to find it. "Plane!" was the announcement if you caught sight of one above. Colin would laugh uproariously if he found one first. It was June, and the grass was thick and cool. I felt such pure happiness, such pure, simple joy.

When I was a little girl, about six or seven, I had a recurring dream that I could fly. In my dreams, I would take off from the roof of our house, and I would fly and feel that soaring, freeing sensation, looking at the neighborhood from the heavens, a rush through my stomach. It was such a happy dream, and it embodies for me a real sense of ecstasy and freedom.

I feel that way at times now. When a day goes well, the boys are content, and I realize that it's going to be okay, I feel I can fly again, transcend it all, soar. Those moments aren't every day. But they are littered throughout our lives like true jewels, precious gemstones, reminding me and reminding us all of the possibility.

Card received on February 2, 1994

My dear Michele,

I know you must feel anxiety about your work. Whatever that portends, we have no control. What does not change is the incredible blessings God has given you. In terms of talent, you are incomparable in an obvious and undeniable way. Your insights and ability to describe those insights in a profound and witty way is something God gives only to a rare few. In terms of our family, we have received all that we could have hoped for and more. Remember that the conception of Weldon was medically iffy.

Please don't get impatient. Your time is now whether your book or telescript or next column gets sold today, tomorrow or next year. Keep your faith in all God has given you. God will always answer your needs. He always has and always will.

I will be with you through it all.

Love.

21

Packing for the Afterlife

It wasn't so much the hundreds, perhaps thousands of photographs chronicling a dozen years of a seemingly happy couple crammed into shelves of photo albums, the wedding video (which I dare not view), the piles of eloquent cards bursting with his everlasting devotion, or the silk ties I gave him that he left behind.

What startled me most was reading the letters I wrote to myself, only for myself, in journals smelling of must and damp from years sequestered. These were journals I started when I could never have imagined the life I was leading now. These were the hieroglyphics of a young woman untouched by violence. They showed me a woman who had tried so hard at being romantic, making it all perfect, having it really be as good as it looked.

Divorce for a woman like me who never dreamed it possible was mountain enough. The admission that I was the victim of domestic violence also seemed insurmountable, but I managed. I am still managing. But the act of physically holding my past in my hands, touching the part of me he worked to eliminate—reading it, viewing it, packing it up, putting it in boxes, wrapping the years, and facing in words the irretrievable promises lost—that got me.

The entries in the black vinyl book bared a young woman—a girl, really—I needed to squint at to recognize. She was rescued from a time so long ago, a place oceans away that I had to strain to recall. I was young then and anything was possible. Anything except this. I quoted D. H. Lawrence, Shakespeare, James Joyce, Albert Camus, and Jackson Browne. On the same page as a Dylan

Thomas poem I quoted Bill Quateman, a local folk singer.

In my journals from high school and college, I wrote about every crush, every career obsession, every mood, every desire to save the world, to understand it, describe it, and feel it with passion, purity, simplicity, innocence, drama.

In the worn pages were poems and charcoal drawings, ink sketches and conversations so raw no one could have understood them but me; all of them were here. I held the evidence in my hands, it must have happened, it must be true. At some time I must have been this naive, this lucky, this blessed. I must not have known what it is to feel trampled. See, there, let me show you, I once had this life that had not been betrayed.

In an envelope along with an old passport were photographs squirreled away of old boyfriends: young faces, some with mustaches, some clean-shaven and fresh, some from college, some after, all from the years before I married. I look at these pictures of kind boys, happy men I could have loved, but didn't marry. I wonder if they, too, would have broken promises or been someone other than who they swore they were. I wonder if they would have ever hit me.

I was uncovering the layers, forced to review it all, packing to move out of the house that we swore would be our last move, the house that would solve all the problems, the house where happiness would last forever. Four years after we bought it and one year after the day I made him leave, it was time for my children and I to leave too.

"Can we please live somewhere Daddy hasn't been?" Weldon asked one day. And I didn't know what to say. But it planted the seed, and months later the seed began to sprout.

I could no longer play those games with myself that living there didn't matter, that I could paint the living room and it would all go away. I was tired from pretending my heart didn't sink when I opened the back door, knowing this is where the dream soured, that corner over there, under the children's coats, where their baseball hats were hanging on wooden coatracks of chickens and cows, where he said those words.

The death words. They were thick, dark, and horrifying, words that make your body instantly grow cold. When I heard those words, I knew my life had been changed forever.

Please, God, let me kill her.

Every inch of the house held a secret, and every ounce of its contents I had to hold in my hands, tangible salutes to what I thought was real, and decide if I wanted to keep it or throw it away. The dream was dead, the plans quashed, and all that was left for me to do was to file it all somewhere; to give away the jewelry box, the crystal angel, the gray dress he gave me but I never liked anyway. I needed to listen to my heart and to my boys, who said they wanted to live somewhere new.

We were moving to a new life, only miles away, to my brother Paul's house near my mother and my sisters. My mother bought the house from my brother, getting a mortgage on her own home, the home she and my father paid cash for twenty years before. We were going to start over, leaving the hurt and the memories on Linden Avenue.

Folding, separating, stacking in boxes, wrapping in newspapers, labeling it all were deliberate, donkey-paced chores that helped me say good-bye. I discarded relentlessly. I resisted the urge to label every box "The Past" and instead used more practical destinations the movers could understand, such as "Family Room" or "Basement." I could have sealed many of the boxes with tape soaked in tears, but I pressed on. I told the boys about their new rooms, their new school, how we would be closer to my mother, my sisters, and not too far from their friends.

My sisters came over to help me pack. Madeleine was ruthless in her dismissal of the past. "Get rid of this," she would say over and over.

I did that thing I always do when it aches to be still; I kept myself incredibly busy for weeks before the move, making moving about what lay ahead, not what I was leaving behind. So I made moving my family away from our past about putting clouds on Brendan and Colin's new bedroom ceiling and sponging Weldon's room pale blue. I made it about organizing the toy boxes when really it was all about making my family full enough with four, where there once were five. And I felt lucky again.

"Govern a family as you would cook a small fish—gently," was a saying I painted in green calligraphy on the walls of the new breakfast room.

Once I live somewhere new, once we all live somewhere new, the memories will die. They won't be stoked daily by walking through a room that has a certain smell, a certain feeling. Was it just last Christmas he hit me? Was it the Christmas before? I wanted us to live somewhere that had no lingering aroma of pain, somewhere the air was not smothered in hurt.

I packed for weeks. The boys were little help, though I let them put their books in boxes and some of their clothes. These couldn't be broken, and I wanted to move to the new house without anything more destroyed. Enough of our lives, enough of my heart already had been.

And then the morning came. While my sisters watched the boys, four men lifted all the contents of every room and loaded it onto a truck. The living room, the family room, the boys' rooms, our old room, the one that had bright orange walls when we'd moved in, the one with valances I covered in ivory silk.

The men carried my life out into the street, loaded it onto a truck, and drove away. In the time it took to watch a movie, my life in this house was gone. Nothing was left but dirt on the carpet and circles of brown packing tape that had been dropped. My shoes clicked on the bare wooden floors upstairs. These were the floors he stripped before we moved in. Here was the carpet we laid in the basement. There was the new wood floor we put in the family room. Bleached oak. I had loved those squares of bleached oak.

Echoing in every room was the lost giggling and the crying from the three years we lived inside these walls. Now empty, the rooms seemed smaller, too small to hold as much hurt as was forced inside them. Too small to make me feel as bad as I did inside them.

The old dream had died. It was time to move away.

I make it sound simple. It was not. It was emotionally draining and hard to physically arrange it all, as I was teaching graduate school and just trying to manage day to day. Financially, my family was incredibly supportive. My mother handled the closing and all the paperwork, and a few days before we moved, my brother Paul handed me a brown manila envelope with the cash needed for the movers. I cried.

All of this was possible because my mother made it so. I moved to the house where my brother Paul and his family had lived for a decade before they moved somewhere new. We moved to a house where my children felt safe and it didn't hurt me to breathe. A house that had only known love in its walls.

I could not change the past, but I could shape the future. I would live with my boys in a house where no one felt afraid. I would make for my boys a home without ghosts, without the shadows of tears and hurt. I would make for my boys a future that did not include violence.

I felt I could only do this somewhere new because the ghosts were terrorizing me. There was the old kitchen with the mice every winter and the family room where the boys played, from which I saw the garage door go up when he got home from work. There was the living room where we had our parties, the last one just a few weeks before he left. There were the birthdays in the basement, the puppet shows for the boys, the Easter Bunny footprints I placed on the living room carpet in baking soda.

There was the feeling that this place would be the last place we moved to and that buying it was the best thing we had ever done. There was the feeling that everything I thought would come true would not.

I packed what was in the closets. I gave him the things he had forgotten: the sailing trophy, the silver pitcher his mother gave him, the photographs of him as a child. I put in boxes the rest of the memories, the moments, the years upon years of lives sewn together, lives now come undone. I buried the wedding pictures in boxes I would not open, boxes I could not open.

This all reminded me of a book Weldon read in second grade about the expedition to uncover King Tutankhamen's tomb. Just as with the Egyptian boy king, part of me had died, part of me could never be revived. It was the innocent part, the wishing part, the part about being twenty-five and thinking your life will proceed as planned, that the books you've read on relationships work, that your life will always be happy, that someone you love won't hurt you. The part of me in the journals on the shelves. The young woman who never dreamed of an unhappy ending. The little girl who had never known sorrow, real sorrow. The little girl who hid under the bed from Richard Speck, after he was caught.

But I packed for a glorious unknown afterlife. I placed in the sacred chambers only the things that would serve us all well, only those things that were about joy and only those things that were not about abuse. I craved an afterlife, a life after the abuse, a life after the tears.

We started in a new house, a house with three bedrooms and a family room painted blue. A few months after we moved in I painted the living room cantaloupe, a tawnier shade than the apricot of the living room on Linden. I painted the dining room a more muted turquoise, a wash really. Because I was more muted. I painted the kitchen pale gray and the breakfast room the same, but with sayings on the wall in dark green script. "Stay, stay at home my heart and rest," by Henry Wadsworth Longfellow was on one wall adjacent to a saying by Aristotle: "Happiness depends upon ourselves."

There comes a time when you are able to pack up the past and move forward, when the future is less about healing and more about dreaming again. And now, we are in a house that holds the afterlife for us, for me.

There is a life after it all, a new life we can shape to resemble the life in new dreams.

Card received on December 16, 1992

Dear Michele,

I want to free that ballerina inside of you. I want to do what I can to make your life a joy. I know it can be and the joy you deserve.
Love.

22

Thanksgiving

Pushing the shopping cart through the crowded aisles at Dominick's with Colin squirming in the front basket, Brendan sitting cross-legged inside the cart, and Weldon hanging onto the front of the cart, facing me, I tried to concentrate on the list. I didn't want to forget anything.

Large frozen turkey, at least ten pounds. Celery. Potatoes, sweet as well as new red. Butter. Rolls. Broccoli—maybe they won't like broccoli. Okay, carrots. Fresh cranberries. Walnuts. A can of mandarin oranges. Yes, and enough lettuce, tomatoes, cucumbers, and croutons to make a marvelous salad. Gooey dressing, not the low-fat kind. Pumpkin pie. Flowers. I didn't even know who would be eating this feast; I only knew it would be important to them. It was very important to me.

It was November 1996, a few days before Thanksgiving. It had been one year since I "graduated" from my group for women recovering from domestic violence at Sarah's Inn. I was ready to go back. I was ready to give back, I thought, to a place that had given so much to me. I could redeem the past by helping a woman who came after me, a woman somewhere behind me in the crowded line.

A dozen of us had spent close to six months every Wednesday evening telling each other our stories. Some stories seemed too painful to hear, let alone bear. Maria had woken up to her husband strangling her in their bed, then she remembered nothing until she awoke in a hospital room weeks later. Her children had been taken away, and she worked for a year to get them back. Betty's husband would come at her with knives. Cheryl's husband followed her to her job as a late-shift nurse and tried to force her off the expressway with his car. Mary's husband broke into her home and started a fire after they were divorced. Anna's husband never hit her, but called her names and belittled her for two decades until she could no longer function or leave the house. Sometimes it hurt just to listen; but we all listened. We shared the same halted past, only altered by circumstance.

I was buying the food for a family at Sarah's Inn, any family. I called the director to say that if it would help, I would be happy to bring the makings of a Thanksgiving dinner over for someone living in temporary housing at Sarah's Inn to prepare. I know that for a woman who has felt the hauntings of abuse, sometimes even the simple act of placing a turkey in an oven is therapeutic.

Concentrating on simple tasks—making cookies, stirring new sauces, placing a roast in the oven—these motions for me were pure and uncomplicated. The tactile distraction of rote efforts was helpful, soothing.

If you cannot control or predict the behavior of someone in your home, at least you can direct the outcome of a loaf of bread. I would play games with a temperamental electric oven, knowing that if the first dozen cookies was placed on the top rack, the bottoms of the cookies wouldn't burn. After the oven was warmed up a half hour or so, the cookie sheets could go on the bottom when the heat would be even. Some days a triumph was defined by bottoms of cookies that weren't black.

The process of mixing and kneading or stirring and adding was quieting to me. When my husband was still living with us, I made dinners with never-tried ingredients, and the boys were eager to sample it all, even if he wasn't there for dinner. I would slice the roasted chicken and fan it out—the way they do in restaurants where the same meal would be $14.95—and garnish with carrots or peas or green beans or whatever I could disguise, dribbling the sauce in that nouvelle, photo-stylist way. One night when he came home from work late, he scraped the entire dinner plate I made for him—without tasting it—into the kitchen garbage can in front of me. He wasn't hungry, he said. He ate at the office.

When I was married to him, simply feeling I had control over a meal was sometimes enough to keep me going. Knowing that I could do that well, that I could add this, sauté that, and it would taste marvelous was enervating. I did anything to combat how he made me feel. I cooked a lot; I baked a lot of bread.

"I hate who I am around you," I told him once. When I am without you, I thought, I am a woman who can do anything.

But on that Thanksgiving Day, 1996, I was imagining a woman who was hurt preparing this feast for her family, and I pictured the smiles and the prayers and the relief. There is majesty in a dinner lovingly prepared, a feast shared with dear, close friends. I wanted this for myself and for another woman like me. I wanted to help her get better. The image filled me, knowing how the preparations created the joy. So I shopped feverishly, the boys rushed and confused.

"I thought you ordered a turkey for Saturday when the cousins would come to our house," Weldon said.

"Yes, yes, yes," I responded, rushed, impatient. "This is a special Thanksgiving dinner for someone else." Who? I don't know. My effort was simple and I feared it was not enough, but it was what I could afford to give.

I asked the young girl bagging the groceries to put everything in a large box. I had picked a frozen fifteen-pound turkey, and I hoped it was enough.

It was cold when we left the store, and the boys were scrambling for hats and gloves and zippers. I didn't feel the cold; my heart was warm. With the boys and the groceries in the station wagon, we headed to Sarah's Inn, about two miles away, the shelter for women that had helped rescue my life.

After pulling to the curb, I lifted the box from the back of the station wagon. I rang the bell and identified myself at the unmarked building, the building with a location each client was sworn to keep secret. There can be no threat of a former partner harming the women or children who come here. Walking up the stairs with my box of provisions, convulsions of sadness filled me.

I reached the landing and told the person at the front desk that I was donating these items to any resident or group of residents who wanted to make a Thanksgiving feast. It was all I could do to put the boxes down before I started to cry. She asked me to write down my name and phone number. I did it hurriedly, and she thanked me.

I ran down the two flights of stairs to the car.

"Mommy, what's the matter?" Brendan asked. "Was someone mean to you?" They seemed to ask that question a lot.

I couldn't explain, and I couldn't stop crying, my breathing shallow and furious. I didn't know why the hurt felt so fresh and new again, but I felt as helpless and as wounded as I did the first night I came to that place more than a year earlier. I didn't know that the pain would continue to come back in fits and starts for years, that it only took the ignition of a memory through some random event to relive it all. That night just by walking into Sarah's Inn after a year's absence made the terror I felt in the fresh aftermath of the abuse come alive.

Perhaps it was the thought that I had not come so far, that I would always be part of the sorrow that surrounds abuse. Perhaps it was because the place was filled with all-new faces, all-new clients, all-new volunteers. It is never over, it is never done. I may no longer be there, but there will always be a thousand, a million, seven million more women like me. There is always a woman who feels the shame, the hurt, the sting. One box of food will never be enough.

I wanted to separate myself, be the removed benefactress and not the victim, not swallowed by the madness, but above it, beyond it. Yet the intense sorrow I felt reminded me that I will always be part of a history of abuse, a history shared with these women whose faces and names I did not know, whom I only idealized in my vision. Perhaps I was not ready to walk back up those steps where my boys were loved and drew pictures, learning to have no shame. Not enough time had passed. With the slightest touch, my wounds could bleed.

That Thanksgiving Day, I celebrated with my sister Mary Pat and her family, and my mother. It was an even year, the years in which he was allowed by the courts to have the boys for the day. On the Saturday after Thanksgiving, I prepared a feast for all my brothers and sisters, our children, and my mother at our house. Thirty-four in all.

I placed a twenty-two-pound turkey in the oven and filled it with dressing I had made with two kinds of bread and croutons, water chestnuts, sausage, mushrooms, celery, onions, and walnuts. The smell that filled the house was rich and thick, a penetrating comfort. Sautéed onions. Roasting turkey. I prayed that the family I had bought the food for felt the same as I did, proud and capable. There was bounty, no more sadness.

It is difficult not to be angry; it is exhausting to look for the good in all that has happened. I cannot say I am glad for it all. Of course I wish it had been different. But it is not. I married a man who was handsome and intelligent, and for that I am grateful because our boys carry these positive traits. With him, in love that was boundless for me, I bore three little boys whose faces are bright and whose energy and affection are limitless.

From loving this man who hurt me, I learned that love is a gift not to be betrayed. By how he treated me I learned to never hurt another. I learned that a marriage is not a balance of extremes and that the price for Saturday mornings of homemade pancakes and hugs need not be Saturday nights—a week, a month, a year later—of trembling in a corner of a room, rolled into a ball, terrified.

The yearning for love and completeness should not overshadow the truth. When a partner writes soulful letters, it should not be as an apologetic, deliberate attempt to tip the scales and mask the effect of words and strikes that are meant to break. Those words, if sincere, should just come as a matter of course. Love need not be an exercise in persuasion. Love should not have a steep price. Love should have no price at all.

As a writer I learned that this deep, paralyzing sorrow can be freeing. I am writing from a different, far deeper place that is much more honest, nonjudgmental. By having been afraid and trapped, I have learned the value of trust.

I no longer wear the daily tears of a woman in shock, a woman freshly betrayed. I only now have to brace myself for the occasional verbal attacks, the aggressive meetings in court, the expensive legal manipulations, the phone conversations that are brittle and unkind, the accusations, and the serial crises connected to a chaotic life. I tend to the aftershocks affecting my children. I make amends.

It does get better. And every day I get better. Not long ago tears stung my cheeks as I repeated over and over, "It is easier to be hit once in a while." No, it is not. It is easier to live without violence and fear. It is easier to be able to hang up a phone, shut the front door, or walk away from someone who once threatened my life.

"You did not just hit your wife," I remember telling my husband that July night after the final blow. "You hit me."

He hit me. And he hit me on purpose.

It seems so obviously absurd, now, but it took me a dozen years to be able to admit that.

He will never hit me again.

Though there are millions of women like me, millions of us who have felt the slaps and the taunts, millions of us who have gripped the edge of the bed at night, we are all worthy and deserving of a better life, a better love. It is better to be alone than to be with someone who aims to harm you. We all know it.

There are blessings in my life I couldn't see until he was gone. It took so much energy to placate him and to maneuver a life around him that I had little time to observe, to be still, to take stock. To see.

My three little boys are open and loving. They play basketball, baseball, soccer, football, and an invented game that requires one brother to lay stomach-first on a skateboard while another brother pulls the rope tied to the front wheel. Oh, yes, and then they let go. They are daring, they are hopeful, they are hopefully unscathed.

Sometimes when they are laughing loud and rolling in the grass in the backyard, I forget for a moment where we have been, where they have been, and that they have memories that are cruel and distant, but cruel nonetheless. When they are reckless and full of mischief, their laughter is so powerful it quiets the monsters in my head.

Forcing my husband away from our family was like pulling a knife out of the wound or extracting a bullet. The extrication was severe and traumatizing, but it was the only way to live, the only way to survive. His absence left a hole, a wound infected with memories bitter and undistilled. But I have found that the wound—no matter how deep—heals, and my life has grown around the place where he had been. All our lives have. I am grateful for that.

I have had to work hard to begin to overcome the weighty grief and guilt I felt for marrying a man who acted violently. I have had to work hard to quiet the blame I assigned myself for giving my sons the legacy of a father who battered their mother. But it was a choice, my choice. I have not completely won that battle. I hope I someday will.

Still, I am grateful I stayed as long as I did. Complicating all the other feelings of remorse and regret, I do not have to contend with any mysterious tugging prompted by, "What if I only had . . ." I know now there is nothing I could ever have done to change him or to change our relationship. I tried it all, I did it all. I even placed a holy medal, one my mother had given me, under the mattress on his side of the bed. It was from the patron saint of lost causes, my mother told me. This qualified. It seemed so voodoo, but I would try anything.

The realization that no matter what I did, no matter how many counselors we saw, that none of it had an impact on his behavior took me almost ten years to see. If we had not been in a counselor's office a few days before the last assault, I probably would still be trying. If I hadn't seen the stark duplicity of his words and his actions, I may have been hurt even more. I may not have survived.

If I had not heard Brendan's quiet question, "Did Daddy hit you?" I would have still thought my cleverness disguised the horror in our home. Still, I would rather live with the conviction that I exhausted all the possibilities than to think that if I had stayed, if I had tried one more time, one more avenue, that I could keep my family whole and healthy, happy and ideal. There could be no more staying. I had to leave. I was willing to try to have a good marriage with him, but I was not willing to die trying.

I am grateful I no longer love him. I am relieved I do not hate him. Though I don't understand him, I know who he is, and I know to protect myself. I know who can help me.

I have no permanent outward scars of the violence I endured, only the tenacious scars in my heart that I trust will eventually fade. The drama of the abuse was curtailed before it escalated to an extreme, before the boys were hurt physically, before I was seriously injured. I am fortunate to have tireless advocates for myself and for my children who continue to champion my right and my children's right to be safe.

In opening my eyes and breaking the silence, I have made friends I never would have known in the brutal shroud of secrecy that was my marriage. I am grateful for the blessings of sympathetic strangers and loving friends who embraced me when I felt I could no longer persevere. I am thankful I was always believed. I was believed by attorneys, judges, counselors, even the court-appointed psychiatrist whom my husband tried to convince it was I who was abusive, not him.

For the hundreds of lessons learned by being married to an enigmatic, complicated man, I am thankful. These are lessons millions of women have learned, that love for another sometimes is undeserved, that sometimes someone who loves you hurts you. I learned that I cannot control or influence someone else's behavior; I can only choose my own path. A husband or a partner is not a project to conquer like an old house in need of renovation or a book that needs to be written.

Laughter has helped me. The love that surrounds my life has allowed me to choose the laughter when sadness threatened to suffocate me. The truth is, I would laugh at times only if to hear that I still could.

How many battered women does it take to change a lightbulb?

Just one. And while she is changing the lightbulb, she will defend her life, care for her children, make a home, build a career, and heal herself at the same time.

For Weldon's ninth birthday, I took four of his friends downtown to Navy Pier to the I-Max theater to see a 3-D movie about the oceans, life in the deep. For the most part, that afternoon was as challenging as trying to keep balls of mercury from rolling out of a dropped test tube. But inside the theater, the boys were still and mesmerized by the huge screen and the sounds of the water that seemed to envelop us.

I was fascinated by a tiny lobster that grew out of its hard shell, struggling to shed it and free himself, taking great pains to thrust the heavy, cumbersome shell aside. While the lobster is performing this feat, he is vulnerable to prey. But soon the lobster grows another shell, the next bigger and stronger.

That is me—that is the promise for any abused woman. We grow out of our shells, the relationships that contain us and keep us small and afraid. And while we are shedding those shells, we are vulnerable and hurt, more tender and susceptible to attack than we have ever been. But then we grow new shells, becoming stronger than we ever were before.

I am grateful that on this odyssey I have earned the right to see clearly and to listen closely to the wisdom of my own heart. Caught in the web of domestic violence, you not only question yourself, but you question basic truths. When faced with so much denial and so many complicated explanations, you try to see from the other's perspective. In trying to be reasonable, I lost the ability to reason.

I don't tell myself that I was not really the victim of domestic violence, but only married to a good man with a bad temper. The truth is, my husband abused me. I was his victim. I no longer shrink from that truth; it is as persistent, as healing, and as ultimately nurturing, as the rain. And I let the rain wash me, the truth heal the anger and the hurt.

What do I know to be true? I ask myself this often, and I heed the answer.

Sadly, mine is an ordinary, very common story. But there is nothing ordinary about me or any woman who has awakened from the nightmare, who has stopped the damning dance with an abuser, who has opened her eyes. My story has a happy ending. I give thanks for that. For every woman—any woman—like me, I pray for the strength to emerge to find her own happy ending.

May we all have cause for endless thanksgiving.

Afterword

I would like to hear from you with your comments about this book. I hope reading this book has helped you or someone you know. If you would like, please write and share with me some of your experiences about your recovery from abuse. I hope the process is healing.

Michele Weldon
P.O. Box 5721
River Forest, IL 60305-5721

About the Author

Michele Weldon has been an award-winning journalist for more than twenty years, with essays, columns, and articles appearing in scores of publications such as the *Chicago Tribune, Los Angeles Times, Parenting,* and *Woman's Day.* An adjunct lecturer for graduate and undergraduate students at her alma mater, Northwestern University's Medill School of Journalism, Weldon lives in the Chicago area with her three sons where she is also a frequent public speaker offering writing workshops as well as seminars on finding the joy in everyday life. She serves on the strategic planning board of Sarah's Inn, a domestic violence services agency, as well as on the board of directors of Tuesday's Child and is a volunteer member of Children's Memorial Guild.

Hazelden Information and Educational Services is a division of the Hazelden Foundation, a not-for-profit organization. Since 1949, Hazelden has been a leader in promoting the dignity and treatment of people afflicted with the disease of chemical dependency.

The mission of the foundation is to improve the quality of life for individuals, families, and communities by providing a national continuum of information, education, and recovery services that are widely accessible; to advance the field through research and training; and to improve our quality and effectiveness through continuous improvement and innovation.

Stemming from that, the mission of this division is to provide quality information and support to people wherever they may be in their personal journey—from education and early intervention, through treatment and recovery, to personal and spiritual growth.

Although our treatment programs do not necessarily use everything Hazelden publishes, our bibliotherapeutic materials support our mission and the Twelve Step philosophy upon which it is based. We encourage your comments and feedback.

The headquarters of the Hazelden Foundation is in Center City, Minnesota. Additional treatment facilities are located in Chicago, Illinois; New York, New York; Plymouth, Minnesota; St. Paul, Minnesota; and West Palm Beach, Florida. At these sites, we provide a continuum of care for men and women of all ages. Our Plymouth facility is designed specifically for youth and families.

For more information on Hazelden, please call **1-800-257-7800.** Or you may access our World Wide Web site on the Internet at **www.hazelden.org.**